CLOSING PRAYERS

Facing the Final Crisis on our Knees

RANDY MAXWELL

Pacific Press®
Publishing Association
Nampa, Idaho | www.pacificpress.com

Cover designer: Gerald Lee Monks
Cover design resources: iStockphoto.com | ChristianChan
Interior designer: Aaron Troia
Interior photos: Getty.com

The author assumes full responsibility for the accuracy of all facts and quotations as cited in this book.

Additional copies of this book are available for purchase by calling toll-free 1–800-765–6955 or by visiting AdventistBookCenter.com.

Library of Congress Cataloging-in-Publication Data

Names: Maxwell, Randy, author.
Title: Closing prayers : facing the final crisis on our knees / Randy Maxwell.
Description: Nampa, Idaho : Pacific Press Publishing Association, [2021] | "We have been told that the final movements on Earth would be rapid ones. What about the final movements of prayer? This book answers the question of how to pray in the last hours of Earth's history." | Summary: "How God's people are to pray in the final crisis"— Provided by publisher.
Identifiers: LCCN 2021037199 (print) | LCCN 2021037200 (ebook) | ISBN 9780816367801 (paperback) | ISBN 9780816367818 (ebook)
Subjects: LCSH: Prayer—Christianity. | End of the world. | General Conference of Seventh-Day Adventists—Doctrines.
Classification: LCC BV210.3 .M3745 2021 (print) | LCC BV210.3 (ebook) | DDC 248.3/2—dc23
LC record available at https://lccn.loc.gov/2021037199
LC ebook record available at https://lccn.loc.gov/2021037200

October 2021

DEDICATION

To my "Usos" and prayer partners, Pastors Nemaia Faletogo, Meshach Soli, Rome Ulia, and Willie Iwankiw.

Pursuing "Greater Things" in the Spirit with you brothers is a joy that words cannot express. Thank you for your love and for always having my back.

#GreaterThings!

ACKNOWLEDGEMENT

If it hadn't been for the "kick in the faith" Dr. Ty-Ron Douglas gave me at a Thai restaurant in Lincoln, Nebraska, this book may never have been written. Thank you, my friend, for challenging me to quit procrastinating and write.

CONTENTS

Introduction: Opening Prayer 7

Part One: It's Me, O Lord, Standing in the Need of Prayer

   1 | Change Me 15

   2 | Search Me 26

   3 | Wake Me 38

   4 | Break Me 50

   5 | Send Me 61

Before You Continue 73

Part Two: Revival Uprisings

   6 | "Good Trouble" 77

   7 | Get Used to Different 90

   8 | Praying for Rain 103

Epilogue: A Closing Thought 115

Discussion Guide 121

OPENING PRAYER

A young man I was praying for yesterday is dead today. He was thirty-eight years old.

Though I'm writing this during what one reporter described as "COVID hell," this young man did not lose his life to the killer virus ravaging our world and nation. It wasn't cancer or accident that claimed his life. He was executed by lethal injection at a state correctional facility for a crime committed twenty years earlier.

Without going into detail, this young man was an accomplice in a capital murder case. Despite appeals for clemency on the part of jurors, a prosecutor in the case, Kim Kardashian West, and even a couple of high-profile lawyers who joined the appeals team at the eleventh hour, the Supreme Court did not intervene. And another casualty of the crime perpetrated twenty years ago was claimed last night.

But in the end, it wasn't death that claimed this young man—it was Christ. There on death row, this prodigal, who had been raised in the church, returned to faith and was born again. He spent the last two decades counseling other young men who were heading down a dark and dangerous path to turn their lives around while there was still time. He was not the same person he was at eighteen years of age.

I watched his clemency video and could see the light of Christ in his eyes. I saw something else too. *Peace.* The peace that passes understanding, even with an execution date looming.

And now, as I write this, knowing that this brother in the Lord, whom I only heard about four days ago, is gone, I wonder about his final moments. As I and others were praying in the closing hours of this young man's life, he surely was petitioning heaven too. What were the prayers he prayed at the end? When you've prayed all kinds of prayers during the course of your life, what prayers do you pray when your time to pray is coming to an end? For this young man, what were his "end-time" prayers?

The question is relevant to us because our world is on its own cosmic "death row" with a Judgment Day looming. How then should we pray?

As I write this, I'm aware of people I have worked with or, by extension, prayed with who are on ventilators, struggling for breath due to coronavirus. I received an email just a few nights ago from the daughter of one of my former publishing house colleagues who was in the ICU with COVID. She was reaching out to me for prayers for her father, and I assure you the nonverbal focus and urgency came through the text loud and clear. Her prayer wasn't about the weather or a blessing on her food, the economy or the status of the latest stimulus package stalled in Congress. Her prayer was specific, pointed, real, and urgent. No time for niceties or generalities when a window of time may be closing for someone you love.

I was privileged to pray with my former workmate twice: the day before he died, and again, just hours before he breathed his last. The first conversation was two-way—me doing most of the talking; he, responding in short, breathless phrases. With the rhythmic whooshing of oxygen machines in the background, I prayed for my friend.

The second call was one-way. His daughter put me on speaker and put the phone to my friend's ear. He was no longer able to speak, but the family felt he was able to hear. Again, I prayed. But this time my prayer was different. I can't tell you what all I said, but I wanted my friend to be assured of God's love for him and his family and of the sure promise of eternal life for all who trust in Him. Believe me when I say that it is an awesome thing to stand between the living and the dead as an intercessor—when your voice is among the last a person will hear in this life.

Three and a half hours later, I received the text message I dreaded. My friend was gone. Mine was a last call.

Earlier that morning, I penned these words in my journal: "Lord,

____________ may be taking his last breaths. What is the conversation You and he are having right now? What is on _________'s heart as he struggles for breath while in the hospital with COVID? I'm sure his prayers are not just for himself but for his wife and children and grandchildren. He is surely placing them in your hands and begging for their comfort and salvation, because that's the man You made him to be."

I have no doubt that my friend is sealed for the resurrection. But what are the prayers of one who faces his mortality, not in theory but in stark reality? Not years from now but moments from now?

Think back over your life of prayer. I suspect you're not too different from me, and you've prayed about everything from pets to parking spaces, money to marriage, jobs to justice, hurt feelings to healings, cancer to court dates, and retirement to revival. I have prayed about pastoral calls, board votes, homes to purchase or rent, disappointments in ministry, suspicious moles that had to be biopsied, questionable mammogram findings in my wife, and for my own daughter and son-in-law as we all grieved the loss of their first child at sixteen months.

And I've prayed for revival—a lot. Starting with *If My People Pray* in 1995, the Lord laid a prayer burden on me to seek His face for revival and to call God's people to the same. And while there is evidence of revival happening in other parts of the world, the spiritual awakening that we've prayed for eludes us here in the western world. In fact, in many places in Europe and America, the church, instead of reviving, is regressing. Like too many COVID patients, the church appears to be transitioning into a palliative rather than a Pentecostal phase.

This is happening at the worst possible time—just before Jesus comes again. At a time when believers need to be most powerful spiritually, we seem to be the weakest. End-time delusions are at an all-time high, and I'm afraid we're blind to the deceptions we're least prepared for—those within our own hearts. How then should we pray? It's that question I seek to answer in this book.

For more than one hundred years, we've been told,

We are living in the time of the end. . . .

The agencies of evil are combining their forces and consolidating. They are strengthening for the last great crisis. Great changes are soon to take place in our world, and the final movements will be rapid ones.[1]

As I write these words, I am nearly numb to the speed of change and chaos. The first strain of the killer coronavirus hadn't been tamed before a new, more aggressive strain appeared on our shores. In a moment of great shame and disgrace, lawmakers huddled in fear on the floor of the Senate chamber as the United States Capitol was stormed by extremists attempting to overturn the 2020 election. Something like that hadn't happened since the War of 1812. The stock market lurches like a drunk person between historic highs and lows. Falsehoods and conspiracy theories blanket the earth at the speed of a tweet, post, or instant message, and something as simple as a mask has divided our country more than any terrorist attack at home or abroad.

> The final crisis we need to be concerned about the most is the crisis of self and surrender to the Holy Spirit.

Great changes are taking place every moment of every day, but are the prayers of God's people keeping up? If the final movements are to be rapid ones, what about the final moves among God's people? How are we to prepare for the final crisis? The last revival? What should God's people be praying about right now in Earth's final hours?

In the sports of basketball and football, there are four quarters or periods of regulation play. The early periods are used for sizing up the opposition, testing their strengths and weaknesses to determine their game plan. At half-time, adjustments are made based on what was learned in the early going. The third quarter is more intense, and the speed of the game accelerates. But it is the fourth and final quarter that is the most important. And in the final two minutes of the last quarter is where most games are won or lost. Here's a critical truth: the plays you call to win the game in the fourth quarter are very different from the ones you call in the first.

I believe the same is true of prayer. The world has entered the fourth and final quarter. In reality, because all the major time prophecies have expired, we're in overtime. And the prayers we pray now to end the "game" in triumph may need to be different from the prayers we've prayed before. It's time to go deep in prayer—not solely for more power to do great exploits for God in ministry but for more humility to allow God to do great exploits of grace and transformation in our hearts. The final crisis we need to be concerned about the most is the crisis of self and surrender to the Holy Spirit. And the current crush of rapid movements unfolding in our world today has revealed the magnitude of this crisis in the hearts, not of sinners, but of saints!

"When the Son of Man comes, will he find faith on the earth?" (Luke 18:8). It's a good question. For sure, He will find injustice on the earth. Without question, He will find racism on the earth. He will surely find pride, protest, corruption, lying, exploitation, covetousness, strife, envy, hatred, and unbelief. But will He find faith among those who "cry out to him day and night" (verse 7)? And what will they be crying out to Him about? That's the discussion I wish to have with you in the pages of this book.

I've wanted to write this book for years now. But it wasn't the right time. In the middle of the pandemic that changed the world, I came upon a short book by Craig Groeschel, titled *Dangerous Prayers*. It struck me as light reading—until I read it. I found myself preaching a series inspired by the prayers he wrote about and added more to the mix. The response to those messages, in context with the times we are living in, signaled the need for a book focused on an end-time prayer strategy: prayers of preparation, examination, awakening, breaking, disturbing, and going.

Among the warriors who joined David at Hebron for the sole purpose of making him king over all Israel were two hundred chiefs and their relatives from the tribe of Issachar. They were described as "men who understood the times and knew what Israel should do" (1 Chronicles 12:32). They knew when to join the fight and what to do when they got there. We need some spiritual sons and daughters of Issachar today—prayer warriors who understand the times and know what to pray in preparation for the coming of King Jesus. Can Jesus count on you?

It's the fourth quarter, my friends. Business as usual is over, which means praying as usual is over. Time to go deep into the final prayers that will defeat the enemy and prepare a people to meet the Lord. In the final hours of Earth's history, it's time to pray the right prayers at the right time in the right way for the right reasons. These I call *closing prayers*.

Shall we pray?

---

1. Ellen G. White, *Testimonies for the Church* (Mountain View, CA: Pacific Press®, 1948), 9:11.

Part One

IT'S ME, O LORD, STANDING IN THE NEED OF PRAYER

I look back over my entries since the coronavirus hit, and I am a mess—up and down, hot and lukewarm, inspired and insipid. That's the journey, isn't it? It's like the prayer by Ted Loder from Guerrillas of Grace:

O Eternal One, it would be easier to pray if I were clear and of a single mind and a pure heart; if I could be done hiding from myself and from you, even in my prayers.

But, I am who I am, mixture of motives and excuses, blur of memories, quiver of hopes, knot of fear, tangle of confusion, and restless with love, for love.

I wander somewhere between gratitude and grievance, wonder and routine, high resolve and undone dreams, generous impulses and unpaid bills.

Come find me, Lord. Be with me exactly as I am. Help me find me, Lord. Help me accept what I am, so I can begin to be yours.

Make of me something small enough to snuggle, young enough to question, simple enough to giggle, old enough to forget, foolish enough to act for peace; skeptical enough to doubt the sufficiency of anything but you, and attentive enough to listen as you call me out of the tomb of my timidity and into the chancy glory of my possibilities and the power of your presence.*

This is me, Your son. I'm a mess, Lord. But I'm Your mess. Please keep me in Your hand, working my clay and fashioning me into a vessel fit for Your glory. Even though I can't seem to get out of my own way and I am bolder in imagination and in my writing or preaching than I am in real life, don't give up on me.

—Randy's journal, 8/14/20

---

* Ted Loder, *Guerrillas of Grace* (San Diego, CA: Lura Media, 1984), 32.

1

CHANGE ME

*"I tell you the truth, no one can see the kingdom of God
unless he is born again."*
—John 3:3

*Christians are as guilty for not having the Spirit,
as sinners are for not repenting.*
—Charles G. Finney

Shock and awe: those were my emotions as I watched coverage of the siege on the United States Capitol during a joint session of Congress to count the electoral votes from the 2020 presidential elections.

Demonstrations were expected. A coup d'état was not. Peaceful protesting in the streets is an American right. Rioting in the Senate chamber, clashing with Capitol police, and vandalizing lawmakers' offices are un-American sedition.

Just six days into the new year, still praying that the dumpster fire that was 2020 was mercifully over, a new horror befell us. Not since the 9/11 attacks on America have I struggled to believe that what I was seeing was real. And yet there it was. Amid the hundreds of images we cannot delete from our minds was that of a makeshift gallows erected opposite the United States Capitol—a hangman's noose framing the dome. The photograph captured other demonstrators holding various banners and signs, including one with two words that seemed profoundly out of place.

Those two words? "Jesus Saves."

It's not that the words aren't true. They are. But in the midst of an insurrection, they seemed less like a call to repentance and more like a call to arms. The rioters adorned with Christian flags and crosses invoked images of the Crusades and called to mind the dark ages of the bloody Inquisition. It didn't help that the Jesus Saves sign was upside down. But why not? Everything else was upside down that day—decency, civility, democracy, and the nationalist form of godliness that denied the power thereof.

Inside the Capitol, lawmakers huddled behind tables and, at one point, were instructed to put on gas masks. Above the roar of confusion, Congresswoman Lisa Blunt Rochester (D-DE) shouted out a prayer while rioters broke through police barriers and into the building.

What prayer do you pray when an unrestrained mob is moments away from breaking through the door where you're sheltering in place? The text of Rochester's prayer, caught on camera from the floor of the House of Representatives, is revealing:

Father God you are all-powerful. We know all things work together for the good. So we trust in you right now in the name of Jesus, that you have this under control.

Right now in the name of Jesus! All things work together, all things!

PEACE! Peace in the land . . . Peace in this country . . . Peace in this world . . .

Lord we ask you for a healing. Right now. Right now in the name of Jesus. Lord protect (unknown) Protect those who are trying to protect us . . .

Protect all of our brothers and sisters in this Congress who protect America Lord.

We just thank you. We praise you. We give you all honor and glory because you are powerful! Above all . . .

We thank you right now. In this MOMENT![1]

It was an extraordinary moment, and it called for an extraordinary prayer—a prayer that, for all anybody in that room knew, could have been the last they would ever hear. A far cry from the innocuous, gender-inclusive intonation offered by a guest chaplain to open the 117th Congress just three days before the riot. That prayer was politically generic and distant. Congresswoman Rochester's prayer was specific and urgently personal. The difference was context: the normalcy of another opening session of Congress versus the abnormality of a seditious siege on Congress. Suffice it to say, you pray differently under fire!

Unprecedented

The year that was looked forward to with such hope and promise as we entered the decade of the 2020s could be summed up by a popular meme, circulating on Instagram and Twitter, of a flying cow seen through the windshield of an anonymous driver. The caption reads, "What the??? Never mind. I forgot it's 2020." In other words, that which would be considered weird, bizarre, or unexplainable under normal circumstances was par for the course in that weird, bizarre, and unpredictable year that was anything but normal.

And the word you heard over and over again to describe all the weirdness of the pandemic, the protests, the violence, the fires, and the politics (don't forget the murder hornets) was *unprecedented*—never before experienced. And yet we continue to experience what has never before been experienced. Amazingly, there is now almost daily precedence for the unprecedented.

Now think with me. What if there was a single word being blasted over and over again on social media and in the streets to describe the church during this unprecedented time of weirdness and upset? What would that word be? I would love to know the words that popped into your mind right now!

Because of this book's focus, you might assume the word would be *prayer*. But some of us have been attending, organizing, and speaking at prayer conferences for thirty-plus years. We have had Daniel fasts; all-night prayer vigils; twenty-four-hour prayer meetings; ten-, thirty-, and forty-days of prayer, and so on. And over the last few decades, we have met and prayed through some other unprecedented times: the 9/11 terror attacks; the great recession of 2008; Hurricanes Katrina, Sandy, and Rita; the pope's address to Congress; the Second Gulf War; the Indonesian tsunami; the mass shootings in Las Vegas; Parkland, Florida; Virginia Tech; Emmanuel Baptist Church; and so on. And while spiritual breakthroughs have happened elsewhere around the world, here in North America, with few exceptions, our prayers have fallen short of producing the revival of true godliness that we've been told is our most urgent need.[2] Why?

Why no revival?

Back in the fall of 2015, I was a passenger in the car of a retired pastor as we drove to Pocatello, Idaho, to conduct some ministry training. He was going to be teaching a class to elders about preaching, and I was going to do a seminar on prayer. As the sagebrush along the interstate whisked by, he suddenly asked me, "So after all the prayer conferences and prayer initiatives over the years, why haven't we seen revival yet?"

The question stung, but I knew what he meant. I cannot remember exactly how I responded to him, but I think we would have to admit that while the idea and the results of revival appeal to us, the means of revival—the prerequisites—do not. We would like an app for that: revival, like Uber Eats, delivered to your door hot and at a time that fits conveniently into your schedule. It's like the poem "$3 Worth of God" by Wilbur Rees:

I would like to buy $3 worth of God, please.
Not enough to explode my soul or disturb my sleep, but just enough to equal a cup of warm milk or a snooze in the sunshine.
I don't want enough of Him to make me love a black man or pick beets with a migrant.
I want ecstasy, not transformation.
I want the warmth of the womb not a new birth.
I want about a pound of the eternal in a paper sack.
I'd like to buy $3 worth of God, please.[3]

But in the closing hours of Earth's history, the days of discounting God are over. *The time is now* to value God properly—to give Him the glory due His name and to repent for trying to have Pentecost without Calvary. Revival without the Redeemer.

Is it possible that in our pursuit of the fruit, we've neglected the Vine? "I am the vine; you are the branches," Jesus said. "If you remain in me and I in you, you will bear much fruit; apart from me you can do nothing" (John 15:5). Fruit is the outcome of a relationship. Pursuing revival without a relationship with the Redeemer is like marrying someone for his money. You love his wealth and the material comforts that wealth provides, but the marriage is simply an arrangement—a means to an end.

Jesus says, "If you abide in Me—remain connected to Me in a saving, intimate relationship—the fruit of revival will naturally come. But apart from this connection to Me, you will be fruitless." Is it possible that in our pursuit of revival, we have left Jesus outside, knocking and seeking entrance into His own church?

I believe in this moment we have been summoned to let Jesus in. God is calling us back to our first love—to return to the basics of our faith and discover again why we are Christians in the first place or if we are indeed Christians.

This is a moment for you and me to do as the apostle Paul says: "Examine yourselves to see whether you are in the faith; test yourselves. Do you not realize that Christ Jesus is in you—unless, of course, you fail the test?"

(2 Corinthians 13:5). The Classic Edition of the Amplified Bible says it this way: "Examine and test and evaluate your own selves to see whether you are holding to your faith and showing the proper fruits of it. Test and prove yourselves [not Christ]. Do you not yourselves realize and know [thoroughly by an ever-increasing experience] that Jesus Christ is in you—unless you are [counterfeits] disapproved on trial and rejected?" (AMPC).

According to Paul, there is a time of testing and examining. And what is being tested is us. If you think that this period of crises—COVID and racial injustice and economic and political instability—is solely a time of judgment and testing for the world that is rejecting Christ, you are mistaken. I believe this current period of crises is equally a time of judgment and testing on the church that claims to represent and follow Christ. After all, who is Paul talking to when he says, "Examine yourselves to see whether you are in the faith"? The world? It's not in the faith. He's talking to those who allegedly have Jesus Christ inside them—unless they are counterfeits, which can only be revealed under testing.

The testing time

We see such testing brought by God on the children of Israel following the deliverance at the Red Sea. God may have taken His people out of Egypt, but He still had to take the Egypt out of them. And the desert was His operating room.

Three days beyond the Red Sea, they reached a place called *Marah*—a word meaning "bitterness." The former slaves were thirsty. The good news for the thirsty people was that there was water at Marah. The bad news was that the water was bitter! It was undrinkable and foul!

Now remember, who led them to Marah? To bitterness? God. And why did He lead them there? Exodus 15:25 says that there He "put them to the test." Deuteronomy 8:2 reveals the nature of the test: "Remember how the Lord your God led you all the way in the wilderness these forty years, to humble and test you in order to know what was in your heart, whether or not you would keep his commands." God led them to Marah to see what was in their hearts.

Nothing reveals what's really in the heart more than life's bitter experiences.

And how did they do on the test? "The people grumbled against Moses, saying, 'What are we to drink?' " (Exodus 15:24). They failed it miserably. They were like the boy who went to his college professor and said, "Professor, I don't believe I deserve this F that you gave me." The professor said, "Son, I don't believe you deserve it either, but it's the lowest grade we had."

Remember, *Marah* means "bitterness." We don't know whether it was called Marah before the children of Israel got there. If it was already known by that name before, maybe they would have expected the waters to be bitter. But maybe it was named Marah after this experience. We don't really know.

What we do know is that the word means "bitterness." But the root word goes even deeper. The root word of *Marah* means "deliberate, defiant, disobedience." Think of a pouting child with pursed lips, squinting eyes, and furrowed brow, whose arms are folded in defiant rage. Maybe you've seen that look in your own children or grandchildren. I know I've seen that face on mine. It isn't pretty.

I remember having to physically remove a young man from a classroom at church after he had caused a disturbance and was verbally abusing others in the class. My wife and I asked him to leave the room. He became *Marah* and refused to leave. After multiple attempts to reason with him, we physically had to pick him up and carry him outside where we could talk more freely and let him know his behavior was unacceptable and that he owed the class an apology.

In the Torah, it says, if you have a son who is *Marah*, you have to stone him. That's how severe *Marah* can be. (Fortunately, we didn't have to go that far with the young man!) It's not just a bitter experience. That's part of it, but along with that bitter experience comes a deliberate, defiant disobedience. It's *Marah*!

People's true characters are not totally revealed until the time that they do not receive what they sincerely believe is rightfully theirs. Do you think you would have responded any differently? How about now? Are you responding differently today?

Through COVID-19, nationalistic unrest unlike we've ever seen, and hate-mongering, the world has been brought to a *Marah* moment. And what is in the hearts of many is being revealed. What's in your heart in this *Marah* moment? If Facebook and Twitter are any indications, then what's in the heart of even God's people is often shameful. *Marah*.

This *Marah* moment is not just about the wickedness and coming judgments on the world—what's happening "out there." It's about the people of God and what's happening "in here." The crisis of the times is revealing what's in our hearts and who bears the Father's name. The question is not—as the Capital One ad campaign asks—"What's in your wallet?" The question for our moment in time is, What's in your heart?

I was reading a blog post by Carey Nieuwhof, titled "Why Attending Church No Longer Makes Sense."[4] In it, the author made a case for the death of churches where attendance is prized over engagement. The blog generated more than two hundred comments. As I read through them, I decided that one of the reasons fewer people are attending church is because of Christians like these who were making comments like the ones I was reading.

In the wake of the Capitol riot as the electoral votes were being ratified, the pastor and founder of Heart of the Father Ministry, Jeremiah Johnson, apologized for making what turned out to be false prophecies regarding the election. He took ownership of his error and made a humble apology. He expected some pushback from those who might be disappointed both with the election outcome and his recantation. What he didn't expect was the demonic rage aimed at him from some of his "Christian" followers:

> **People's true characters are not totally revealed until the time that they do not receive what they sincerely believe is rightfully theirs.**

After publicly repenting on January 7th, I fully expected to be called a false prophet, etc., in some circles but I could have never dreamed in my wildest imagination that so much satanic attack and witchcraft would come from charismatic/prophetic people. I have been flabbergasted at the barrage of continued conspiracy theories being sent every minute our way and the pure hatred being unleashed.

To my great heartache, I'm convinced parts of the prophetic/charismatic movement are far SICKER than I could have ever dreamed of. I truthfully never realized how absolutely triggered and ballistic thousands and thousands of saints get about . . . [the election]. It's terrifying! It's full of idolatry![5]

It's *Marah.* Some believers think that if they've been hurt or if someone disagrees with them, they get a pass to lash out with cutting words and scathing rebukes. But the Bible gives no such pass. The Word says, "In your anger do not sin" (Ephesians 4:26). It also says to "get rid of all bitterness [*Marah*], rage and anger" (verse 31). Today's default setting for attitudes outside and even inside the church is *rage*. And prayer, no matter how sincere, cannot survive in that atmosphere.

God brought Israel to the place of bitterness on purpose. The test was part of His plan to train them, under comparatively easy circumstances, for the experiences they would face in Canaan. They needed faith in smaller matters so they would have faith in larger matters later.

Sound familiar? "The 'time of trouble, such as never was,' is soon to open upon us; and we shall need an experience which we do not now possess and which many are too indolent to obtain."[6] If we can't trust God now, when things are comparatively easy, how about later? "If you have raced with men on foot and they have worn you out, how can you compete with horses? If you stumble in safe country, how will you manage in the thickets by the Jordan?" (Jeremiah 12:5).

God's purpose in bringing His people to the wilderness was the same as it is for us—to prepare a people to be His bride and to live with Him forever. But the bride of Christ must have the mind and heart of Christ before the wedding. Obtaining these requires nothing less than rebirth. And so, one of the closing prayers you and I must pray before we cross over into heavenly Canaan is the prayer, "Change me."

Have you been born again?

"Very truly I tell you," Jesus said to Nicodemus, "no one can see the kingdom of God unless they are born again" (John 3:3). Have you been born again? Have I? This was the simple and often offensive question that helped spark the Shantung Revival in northern China from 1927 to 1937. The revival was birthed in a time of military conflict, social instability, and lukewarmness in the church. Here's a snapshot of the state of the work in the northern China Mission at that *Marah* moment:

- There was a mass exodus of missionaries due to discouragement.
- Evangelists gave discouraging reports of work among cold, apathetic, and "dead" churches.
- In the northern China Mission at least seventy churches had "died." Many had accepted God's grace as an outside coating of whitewash but had only "covered" their sins, not received forgiveness.
- A discouraged Chinese evangelist reported that more than a thousand people had been converted to Christianity, not to Christ. (A situation all too common today.)

Into this scene of despair came a small Norwegian Evangelical Lutheran woman named Marie Monsen. In her quiet but probing way, she visited mission stations and churches, giving her testimony and speaking on the seriousness of sin. There was no sensationalism. One missionary wrote, "Miss Monsen herself is one of the quietest speakers I ever heard. There was very poor singing, and no invitation for public decisions."[7]

After each service, the diminutive woman greeted the Chinese and missionaries alike with the probing question, "Have you been born again?" The question insulted some and angered others. But she spared no one, asking preachers, deacons, missionaries, and others the same question. When their anger subsided, the Holy Spirit began to search hearts. People discovered and admitted they had not been born again.[8]

The heart searching sparked by Miss Monsen's question produced soul grief and repentance before God that gave way to revival. Revival prayer meetings sprang up not only in churches but also in schools, hospitals, and seminaries. Students in one school began confessing their sins, and the school was closed to allow the revival to have free rein. Services were held every day, morning and evening. At the end of ten days, six hundred girls and nine hundred boys were saved. Miracles occurred, and eventually, the estimate was that there was at least one Christian in each of the one thousand homes in the town.

The revival started with a simple question of self-examination that, at first, caused offense. Spiritual pride prevented people from seeing the reason for the question. After all, they were missionaries! They were suffering from spiritual *anosognosia*—also called "lack of insight." *Anosognosia* is a symptom of severe mental illness that is connected to anatomical damage in the part of the brain involved with self-reflection. This impairs a person's ability to understand and perceive his or her illness. It is the single largest reason why people with schizophrenia or bipolar disorder refuse medications or do not seek treatment. Without awareness of the illness, refusing treatment appears rational—no matter how clear the need for treatment might be to others.

Today's Laodiceans must suffer from this mental illness as well because they lack self-awareness of their condition, thinking they are rich and increased with goods, having need of nothing, and not having a clue that they are, in fact, wretched, miserable, poor, blind, and naked (Revelation 3:17). Their lack of awareness is why Jesus is on the outside trying to get in. My friends, at this critical hour, we must pray continually to be born again, to receive new minds and hearts, and *let Jesus in!*

Necessary change

Why does revival tarry? Perhaps we need to start with the simple question: Have you been born again? Have you settled for church instead of change? And if your first response is, How much change are we talking about? I'll answer that by asking, How much change is required for a caterpillar to change into a butterfly? Metamorphosis is pretty dramatic, wouldn't you say? So is the second birth. It's more than just a little tune-up on our personalities. We must have new DNA, new hearts, and new minds.

How much change are we talking about? Your first clue is found in the words of Jesus: "Whoever wants to be my disciple must deny themselves and take up their cross and follow me" (Mark 8:34). The change Jesus is talking about requires a death to self and a new creation. It requires a new way of seeing, a new way of thinking, a new way of being, and yes, a new way of praying. Prayer that responds to the simple yet profound question, Have I been born again?

Don't take offense. Take stock. The coup d'état most needed today is the one on the capitol of our own hearts. Self must be deposed, so the King of glory can come in.

> Who is this King of glory?
>   The LORD strong and mighty,
>   The LORD mighty in battle. . . .
> Who is he, this King of glory?
>   The LORD Almighty—
>   he is the King of glory (Psalm 24:8, 10).

Our King is about to return. The everlasting doors are poised to open. "However, when the Son of Man comes, will he find faith on the earth?" (Luke 18:8). Will He find those who were willing to choose change over church? Those who wanted more than three dollars' worth of God? Those who wanted the Vine even more than the fruit? Those who were truly born again?

The answer is directly related to your willingness to pray one of the most important closing prayers we could pray: *Change me!*

Closing Prayer

Lord, change me. I ask to be born again. "Take my heart; for I cannot give it. It is Thy property. Keep it pure, for I cannot keep it for Thee. Save me in spite of myself, my weak, unchristlike self. Mold me, fashion me, raise me into a pure and holy atmosphere, where the rich current of Thy love can flow through my soul."[9] Amen.

My Closing Prayer

Write yours here: ____

____

____

____

____

1. "Congresswoman Pleads for God to Heal America During Capitol Riots," Christian News Now, January 11, 2021, https://christiannewsnow.com/congresswoman-pleads-for-god-to-heal-america-during-capitol-riots/.

2. Ellen G. White, *Selected Messages*, bk. 1 (Washington, DC: Review and Herald®, 1958), 121.

3. Wilbur Rees, "$3.00 Worth of God," quoted in Charles R. Swindoll, *Improving Your Serve* (Waco, TX: Word, 1981), 29.

4. Carey Nieuwhof, "Why Attending Church No Longer Makes Sense," *Carey Nieuwhof* (blog), July 17, 2017, https://careynieuwhof.com/why-attending-church-no-longer-makes-sense/.

5. Jeremiah Johnson, quoted in Jessica Lea, "Ministry Leaders Apologize for Prophesying Trump Win," ChurchLeaders, January 12, 2021, https://churchleaders.com/news/388444-jeremiah-johnson-prophesying-trump.html.

6. Ellen G. White, *The Great Controversy* (Mountain View, CA: Pacific Press®, 1950), 622.

7. C. L. Culpepper, *The Shantung Revival* (Atlanta, GA: Crescendo Pub., 1976), 11.

8. Culpepper, 10.

9. Ellen G. White, *Christ's Object Lessons* (Washington, DC: Review and Herald®, 1941), 159.

2

SEARCH ME

Search me, God, and know my heart;
test me and know my anxious thoughts.
See if there is any offensive way in me,
and lead me in the way everlasting.
—Psalm 139:23, 24

If the human heart is the most deceitful of all things,
then the greatest deception we need protection from
is not coming from the left or the right . . . but from within*!*
—Page 34

A news notification that lit up my phone screen caught my eye: "How QAnon Uses Religion to Lure Unsuspecting Christians."[1] In the article, Daniel Burke, the CNN Religion editor, tells how a recently retired Southern Baptist pastor was scrolling through some Facebook posts and came across an unfamiliar hashtag: #WWG1WGA. The retired minister started looking into it online and doing some research. It didn't take long for him to find the hashtag's meaning: "Where We Go One We Go All." It's one of several mottoes used by QAnon—a collective of online conspiracists.

"Q" is an anonymous online persona who claims to have access to classified military and intelligence operations. Since its inception in 2017, QAnon has quickly spread, infiltrating American politics, internet culture, and now, religion. "During the pandemic, QAnon-related content has exploded online, growing nearly 175% on FaceBook and nearly 63% on Twitter, according to a British think tank."[2]

But what is QAnon's appeal to Christians? It is a conspiracy factory, churning out theories with apocalyptic overtones that play into the fears and frustrations of many. The group uses emotionally charged topics, such as child sex trafficking, to draw Christians to the movement. QAnon's seamless blend of Christianity and nationalism, its promise of spiritual knowledge and the primacy of Scripture, and finally, people's desire to evangelize friends and family make it a quasi-religion.

Brian Friedberg, a researcher at the Harvard Kennedy School of Government, is quoted as saying, "This is an information operation that has gotten out of the direct control of whoever started it. . . . It's an operation," he added, "that likely would not exist in a less polarized, confusing and frightening time."[3]

The retired pastor mentioned at the beginning of the article looks forward to a Great Awakening. The pastor said it wouldn't be like the other Great Awakenings, the religious revivals that torched through early America. This one, he said, will concern the state, not the church.

And that should get your attention. A religious revival resulting in state-enforced compliance is what our denomination and many other students of prophecy have long seen in the lamblike beast who speaks like a dragon in Revelation 13. "Then I saw a second beast, coming out of the earth. It had two horns like a lamb, but it spoke like a dragon. It exercised all the authority of the first beast on its behalf, and made the earth and its inhabitants worship the first beast, whose fatal wound had been healed. . . . It deceived the inhabitants of the earth" (Revelation 13:11–14).

Be careful about the source of religious awakenings. Not all revivals are equal.

Notice it is a worship mandate, not a civil rights, public health, or environmental mandate. This is a civil governmental power enforcing the religious practice of worship. And it is a deception that sweeps up the whole earth. My warning to all in this closing hour of Earth's history is, *be careful about the source of religious awakenings.* Not all revivals are equal. Real revival always begins at the house of God.

"It is only as the law of God is restored to its rightful position that there can be a revival of primitive faith and godliness among His professed people."[4] If the coming Great Awakening that QAnon and this pastor are looking for bypasses the church and is not like those that torched through early America, what kind of awakening is it? Describing those earlier revivals, Ellen White writes:

Revivals brought deep heart-searching and humility. They were characterized by solemn, earnest appeals to the sinner, by yearning compassion for the purchase of the blood of Christ. Men and women prayed and wrestled with God for the salvation of souls. The fruits of such revivals were seen in souls who shrank not at self-denial and sacrifice, but rejoiced that they were counted worthy to suffer reproach and trial for the sake of Christ. Men beheld a transformation in the lives of those who had professed the name of Jesus. The community was benefited by their influence. They gathered with Christ, and sowed to the Spirit, to reap life everlasting.[5]

If these are missing from any revival to come, then what kind of revival would that be? *One that deceives the whole earth?* One that has a Christlike veneer that hides the heart of a dragon? One that, if it were possible, would deceive the very elect?

End-time delusions

Not long ago, I was invited to speak at a prayer rally organized by the Pacific Union Conference. It was a global appeal for prayer inspired by the call recorded by the prophet Joel. "Blow the trumpet in Zion, declare a holy fast, call a sacred assembly" (Joel 2:15).

Several days before the event, I was praying, writing in my journal, and wrestling with God over why revival tarries.

> Lord, I need a breakthrough in my own life and walk. I seem no closer to revival than I was in 1995 or 2000. Maybe I was closer then than now. At least then, my focus was locked in on revival. Maybe that's the problem. We've pursued the fruit and not the Vine. Maybe if we concentrated on the Vine—abiding in You—the fruit of revival would naturally come. We want power for a finished work when we haven't submitted fully to the finished work You're doing in us. I'd rather do for You than submit to You. Help me to listen. Would You share with me why revival tarries?

Even as I was writing those words in my journal, I looked up and saw a book on my shelf that immediately grabbed my attention. The title on the book's spine was *End Time Delusions* by Steve Wohlberg. I pulled it from the shelf and quickly flipped to the back cover to remind myself of its contents. "Will Christians vanish in a rapture? Will seven years of apocalyptic terror overtake those left behind? Will one future Mr. Diabolical—the antichrist—rise to control the world? Will he enter a rebuilt Jewish temple, claiming to be God? Will Earth's nations attack Israel at Armageddon?"[6]

After reflecting on those questions, I continued in my journal: "When it comes to end-time delusions, we usually think of spiritualism, false revivals, false sabbaths, false Christs, the rapture, etc. But I wonder if the delusions we should most worry about are those laid out in Matthew 24–25."

The delusion of normalcy

"As it was in the days of Noah, so it will be at the coming of the Son of Man. For in the days before the flood, people were eating and drinking, marrying and giving in marriage, up to the day Noah entered the ark; and they knew nothing about what would happen until the flood came and took them all away. That is how it will be at the coming of the Son of Man. . . .

"Therefore, keep watch, because you do not know on what day your Lord will come" (Matthew 24:37–39, 42).

On the opposite end of the conspiracy bias is the normalcy bias. As in the days of Noah, everyone today is going about business as usual, even in the most unusual of circumstances. A case in point was when I had to fly to Los Angeles to attend that prayer rally I mentioned earlier. My wife, Suzette, was with me, and it was our first flight during the pandemic. I would describe the whole experience as weird, even creepy. So empty. It felt apocalyptic, yet the few people who were at the airport were going about their routine business. You could see the effect of the pandemic, but there was still a sense of normalcy in the abnormal. And today we're no more ready for God's judgment than were the antediluvians before the judgment of the Flood. But normalcy at the end of time is a delusion.

The delusion of hypocrisy and lack of love

"Who then is the faithful and wise servant, whom the master has put in charge of the servants in his household to give them their food at the proper time? It will be good for that servant whose master finds him doing so when he returns. Truly I tell you, he will put him in charge of all his possessions. But suppose that servant is wicked and says to himself, 'My master is staying away a long time,' and he then begins to beat his fellow servants and to eat and drink with drunkards. The master of that servant will come on a day when he does not expect him and at an hour he is not aware of" (Matthew 24:45–50).

This servant professed to be waiting for Christ—outwardly devoted to the service of God but inwardly he has a heart yielded to Satan. It's hard to tell at first. Wheat and tares look a lot alike until harvesttime.

The twenty-eight years we lived in Idaho provided us with a greater understanding of the dynamic between wheat and tares. Wheat fields are abundant in the Treasure Valley of southern Idaho, and when the wheat is growing in its early stages, it's green. But as harvesttime approaches, the wheat matures, and the fields begin to glow with a beautiful straw-gold hue. That's when the tares reveal themselves. As the wheat around them turns gold, the tares (weeds) remain green, sticking out like sore thumbs. In the beginning, it's easy for the tares to blend in with the wheat, but eventually, the nature of the tare reveals what it really is.

The delay of Christ's coming and the destabilization of society are exposing what we're made of—what's in the heart—and it's not pretty. "Selfishness, worldly pride, and ambitions predominate. Fearing that his brethren may stand higher than himself, he begins to disparage their efforts and impugn their motives. Thus, he smites his fellow servants."[7] And this was written before Twitter! How we beat one another down with our texts, tweets, and posts.

The delusion of religion without relationship

Matthew 25:1–13 is the parable of the ten virgins. Please note that the parable is about virgins, not prostitutes. In the book of Revelation, there are two women who play key roles in the end times. One woman is "clothed with the sun, with the moon under her feet and a crown of twelve stars on her head" (Revelation 12:1). This pure woman represents the church, who later fled into the wilderness to escape the persecution of the dragon (see verses 13–17).

In contrast, the other woman is impure.

The woman was dressed in purple and scarlet, and was glittering with gold, precious stones and pearls. She held a golden cup in her hand, filled with abominable things and the filth of her adulteries. The name written on her forehead was a mystery:

BABYLON THE GREAT
THE MOTHER OF PROSTITUTES
AND OF THE ABOMINATIONS OF THE EARTH
(Revelation 17:4, 5).

This impure woman represents a false church that persecutes the saints and seduces the whole earth.

The bridesmaids in Matthew 25 are virgins, not harlots. They represent the people of God at the end of time, who are waiting for the Bridegroom to come. Their virginity is a symbol of their pure doctrine. False teaching is not the issue in this parable.

There's a delay in the bridegroom's arrival, and during that delay, they all sleep, so sleeping is not the issue. At midnight, the call goes out that the bridegroom is coming. All ten maidens awake, and they all have the same lamps. The only difference is that five of these virgins (with pure doctrine) had the wherewithal to bring extra oil to provide for the delay and keep their lamps burning. These five were able to go into the wedding banquet.

The other five virgins (with pure doctrine) did not prepare for the emergency. They took only the amount of oil that would have been sufficient in a best-case scenario: if there had been no delay. We know that the Word of God is a lamp for our feet and a light on our path (see Psalm 119:105). But without the Holy Spirit (the "oil") to illuminate and make the Word real in our lives, all we have is the letter of the law and not the spirit. And Paul says, "The letter kills, but the Spirit gives life" (2 Corinthians 3:6). The lamp without oil is the Bible without Christ; the letter without the Spirit.

These foolish virgins (with correct doctrine) have religion, but they don't have a relationship. That is verified when they finally come to the wedding banquet only to hear the host say, "I don't know you" (Matthew 25:12). There was no relationship. The end-time delusion that we must avoid is thinking that knowing truth is the same as knowing Jesus. But you don't know Jesus until His truth changes you.

The delusion of sloth and fruitlessness

Matthew 25:14–30 illustrates the delusion that Christianity is a spectator sport—I can sit and do nothing with the privileges and gifts given to me by the Spirit. But faith without works is dead (James 2:26). You can't just continue to take in the blessings of God and consume them for yourself. He has given you His blessing, His salvation, the Holy Spirit, the Word of

God, the whole kingdom of heaven, and you're not going to do anything with them? That's a delusion.

The delusion of downplaying injustice and a lack of compassion

Some think that social justice is a distraction from our prophetic mission. The parable in Matthew 25:31–46 reveals that true social justice is directly connected to our mission and to our preparation for Jesus to come. Note that in this final judgment scene, there is no questioning about doctrine here, only compassion. "I was hungry and you gave me something to eat, I was thirsty and you gave me something to drink, I was a stranger and you invited me in, I needed clothes and you clothed me, I was sick and you looked after me, I was in prison and you came to visit me" (verses 35, 36).

The surprise of the judgment is what is brought as evidence before the court. The evidence presented is justice and compassion rendered to our fellow beings—not our Sabbath keeping or veganism.

These delusions, including the Laodicean delusion of comfort-zone Christianity, are more likely to trip me up than belief in the rapture or being fooled by a fake christ.

Closing prayers to avoid end-time delusions

So how do we avoid these and other end-time delusions? To the prayer "Lord, change me," we must add this prayer: "Lord, search me."

Much of what follows in this and the next three chapters was inspired by the book *Dangerous Prayers* by Craig Groeschel. When I first got the book, I thought it was going to be about praying for courage to do great exploits for God. I wasn't expecting it to be about praying for courage to let God do a great work of renewal in me. The subtitle should have given me a clue: "Because Following Jesus Was Never Meant to Be Safe." That was like a sign shouting, "Reader, be warned! Contents may be hazardous to your complacency." Well, I read the book anyway, and true enough, my complacency took a hit. But it was exactly what I needed, and it led me to my own wrestling with the prayers I believe we need to be praying right now—before Jesus comes. But be warned: the following prayers may be hazardous to your complacency.

Still with me? Good. Let's go.

Search me, God, and know my heart;
    test me and know my anxious thoughts.
See if there is any offensive way in me,

and lead me in the way everlasting (Psalm 139:23, 24).

This psalm, attributed to David, ends the way it begins—with the word *search*. "You have searched me, LORD, and you know me" (verse 1). Verse 23 is a bold invitation for God to open the closets and see what skeletons fall out. This is how we need to pray if we're going to avoid end-time delusions.

David, being a shepherd, understands the inspection process of the flock, which is a nighttime ritual known as "passing under the rod." One by one, each lamb would come under the shepherd's rod for review. Each would feel the shepherd's hands and hear his voice speaking its name. It was an individual and intimate examination performed by the shepherd so that the sheep could rest in peace. Under the rod of examination, ticks could be removed, cuts anointed with oil, thorns removed from hooves, and so on.

This describes an external examination. But David gets dangerous and asks for an internal exam of his thoughts and motives.

Not long ago, I replaced a vehicle that I had owned for fifteen years. It looked pretty decent on the outside, but I knew it was on the verge of collapse on the inside. I wanted to find its trade-in value, so I took it to CarMax for an appraisal. An appraisal at CarMax is an interesting experience—especially during the pandemic.

A two-person appraisal team met me at the car and asked me to open the trunk, hood, and all the doors and to start the engine. I did so and was asked to step away. While the car is running, the inspectors, armed with a notepad and flashlight, begins the examination. Under the hood—scratch, scratch, scratch on the notepad. Under the carriage, on their knees— scratch, scratch, scratch on the notepad. Inside the doors, inside the trunk, the interior, and all the while writing notes on that pad. It's a thorough examination, and the whole time I was a bit nervous to know what they were writing. It felt like Judgment Day for my 2001 Dodge Stratus!

That's the kind of inspection David is asking for—one that goes deep. "Search me, God!"

Wanting to honor God in every aspect of his being, David prays for complete, four-level testing: (1) heart, (2) fears, (3) sin, and (4) leading.

Heart: *"Search me, God, and know my heart"*

During a Zoom Bible study class connected to our radio ministry,* I asked

---

* *Hope for Today* is aired on Saturdays and Sundays at 8:00 A.M. on KGNW 820AM, THE WORD, Seattle, WA. Visit www.thewordseattle.com/radioshow/8261.

the question, "What are some subtle ways you embrace evil?" After some nervous silence, someone said, "Evil TV programs." Someone else said, "Movies." But I wouldn't let them off the hook so easily. You see, it's fairly easy to keep our externals in check. But it's the things we think—the things nobody will ever see and the things I will never say out loud—that need to come "under the rod" of God's Word.

> If the human heart is the most deceitful of all things, then the greatest deception we need protection from is not coming from the left or the right or from the media but from *within*!

Why do we need our hearts examined? I like the way the New Living Translation renders Jeremiah 17:9: "The human heart is the most deceitful of all things, and desperately wicked. Who really knows how bad it is?" Listen carefully. The first warning Jesus gave the disciples about the end times was, "Watch out that you are not deceived" (Luke 21:8). If the human heart is the most deceitful of all things, then the greatest deception we need protection from is not coming from the left or the right or from the media but from *within*! Without Christ, your heart is deceitful. You will lie to yourself. We can't afford that end-time delusion. A closing prayer in preparation for the final crisis doesn't just ask God to do something *for* you; it asks Him to reveal something *in* you. Ask God to search your heart.

Fears: "Know my anxious thoughts"

What scares you the most? Aging? Illness? Being alone? Unemployment? David wanted to share his worst fears with God—to face them and give them a name. Craig Groeschel says that what we fear matters, and he made this powerful observation: "What I feared the most revealed where I trusted God the least."[8]

To please God, to serve Him, to honor Him, to live for Him, you cannot be driven by fear. You must be led by faith. "God has not given us a spirit of fear and timidity, but of power, love, and self-discipline" (2 Timothy 1:7, NLT).

Faith doesn't mean you don't get afraid. Faith means you don't let fear stop you. Make no mistake; these are frightening times. You will feel fearful, but you won't let fear paralyze you. So you pray, "Know my anxious thoughts," because what God reveals will show you where you're trusting God the least and where you need to trust Him more.

Sin: "See if there is any offensive way in me"

This is dangerous because it may expose a cherished idol—something you've rationalized. And we all are very good at rationalizing those sins we like or feel we have a right to commit. I've heard people say, "If I've been hurt, I have the right to hurt back!" No, you don't! What Bible are you reading from?

Jesus said, "You have heard that it was said, 'Eye for eye, and tooth for tooth.' But I tell you, do not resist an evil person. If anyone slaps you on the right cheek, turn to them the other cheek also. And if anyone wants to sue you and take your shirt, hand over your coat as well. If anyone forces you to go one mile, go with them two miles. Give to the one who asks you, and do not turn away from the one who wants to borrow from you" (Matthew 5:38–42).

Not in our cancel-culture times, right? Believe me; it wasn't popular when Jesus said it either. In what circumstances have you defended yourself or told others, "Don't judge me"? We need God's help to see the sin that's difficult to see in the mirror. Otherwise, we'll have a blind spot like the people David described:

> In their own eyes they flatter themselves
> too much to detect or hate their sin.
> The words of their mouths are wicked and deceitful;
> they fail to act wisely or do good (Psalm 36:2, 3).

Craig Groeschel discovered that when he's defensive, that's an indication he needs to pay close attention and be open to what God wants to show him. "I've found that the more convinced I am that I'm right about something, the more likely that I'm wrong."[9]

Think about it. The Jewish religious leaders rationalized killing the Messiah! Believe me; we are amazingly capable of rationalizing anything and making it OK. You can't rid yourself of sin. Let God do that.

Leading: "Lead me in the way everlasting"

This is where it gets real. It's a prayer to do the one thing we resist most—change. Are you prepared to hear and act on what God may ask you to do? Do you have the faith to ask and the courage to obey? More than just showing us the impurity of our hearts, more than simply knowing our fears and anxieties, more than knowing how we offend God, we get even more dangerous by asking God to lead, direct, and change us to become who He wants us to be.

"Search me" is a simple but dangerous closing prayer. And our refusal to pray it may be one of the main reasons why revival tarries. I want to challenge you to pray this closing prayer this week. Keep a journal. Write down the four levels of inspection: heart, fears, sin, and leading. Then ask God every day, What's in my heart, Lord? What am I afraid of? Where's the sin in my life that I'm holding onto? Where am I deluding myself? And then ask, What do You want me to do? Where do You want to take me with this? Write what you hear God saying to you.

This is how to pray and prepare for the coming crisis. At the Zoom Bible study, we talked about how we grow bored with the gospel. It happens by not sharing it and not experiencing it on a real level. Praying the way David did in Psalm 139 will keep you alive and safe from end-time delusions. This is how revival comes—from the seeds of repentance.

Closing Prayer

Father God, it's a simple prayer. It looks simple, but it is profoundly dangerous because it challenges me where I live. And before You come again, Lord, it's not just correct doctrine You are looking for. There are a lot of people with correct doctrine who do not know You. You want all of me—my heart as well as my mind. I believe You are coming soon, so I can't afford to play games. I'm asking You to search me. Let me pass under the rod of Your inspection without fear because You are the Good Shepherd. You have given Your life for the sheep—me. For all of my missteps and for all of the foolishness that makes me prone to wander, I thank You for laying down Your life so that I can walk in freedom. Thank You for caring enough to confront me where I need confronting and for removing any self-delusions that could keep me from truly knowing You. Search me, O God, and bring revival in my life. I ask it in Jesus' name. Amen.

My Closing Prayer

Write yours here: ____

____

____

____

1. Daniel Burke, "How QAnon Uses Religion to Lure Unsuspecting Christians," CNN News, October 15, 2020, https://www.cnn.com/2020/10/15/us/qanon-religion-churches/index.html.

2. Burke, "How QAnon Uses Religion."

3. Brian Friedberg, quoted in Burke, "How QAnon Uses Religion."

4. Ellen G. White, *The Great Controversy* (Mountain View, CA: Pacific Press®, 1950), 478.

5. White, *The Great Controversy*, 462.

6. Steve Wohlberg, *End Time Delusions* (Shippensburg, PA: Destiny Image, 2004), back cover.

7. Ellen G. White, *Testimonies for the Church* (Mountain View, CA: Pacific Press®, 1948), 5:102.

8. Craig Groeschel, *Dangerous Prayers* (Grand Rapids, MI: Zondervan, 2020), 40.

9. Groeschel, 52.

3

WAKE ME

"Why are you sleeping?" he asked them.
"Get up and pray so that you will not fall into temptation."
—Luke 22:46

There is nothing more tragic than
sleeping through a revolution.
—Martin Luther King Jr.

You've probably heard or seen the joke often attributed to Will Rogers: "When I die, I want to die like my grandfather who died peacefully in his sleep. Not screaming like all the passengers in his car." That's funny as a joke. Not so much as a commentary on real life in these last days.

I remember driving with my wife and daughters up the California coastline on Highway 1 following a speaking engagement at the Soquel camp meeting. We had spent the previous evening at an amusement park nearby, where my girls had goaded me onto a ride called the Tornado. I know what you're thinking: *Why would any sane person get on a ride with the name* Tornado? I asked myself the same question then, and I still do all these years later.

While my kids laughed and squealed in delight, I was in absolute misery as the world around me literally flashed before my eyes—faster and faster until I felt like everything I'd ever eaten was about to paint everyone around me. The ride mercifully stopped, but not the one in my inner ears. Twenty-four hours later, I was still riding the Tornado, and the snakelike curves of Highway 1 were not making me feel any better. Anyone who has driven that coastal highway knows it is one of the most picturesque drives in the country. But Tornado survivors don't care about the scenic views. I just wanted the spinning to stop. My family was blissfully asleep in the car, unaware of my battle to hold down my lunch.

Finally, I couldn't take it any longer. I saw a gravel turnout and swerved into it, braking to a halt. Suzette felt the sudden drop in momentum and jerked awake just in time to see the Pacific Ocean filling the front windshield. She screamed like the grandfather's passengers, thinking I had fallen asleep at the wheel and driven us off a cliff. Luckily for my family, I was only too awake. Unluckily for me, I was too sick to continue driving.

But doesn't life often feel that way? The world seems to sleep in blissful ignorance while driving off the cliff of sin. Or is it the other scenario? Are Christians asleep in the tornado of events swirling around us while the world screams in terror: "people fainting from fear and expectation of the [dreadful] things coming on the world; for the [very] powers of the heavens will be shaken" (Luke 21:26, AMP)?

To even ask the question reveals the reason why these closing prayers are so important. They are prayers that invite investigation, surrender, and doing the one thing none of us likes to do—change. And why do we need to pray such prayers? Two reasons: first, to clear the way for a revival of primitive godliness, which we need so desperately.

Listen to this: "Before the final visitation of God's judgments upon the earth there will be among the people of the Lord such a revival of primitive godliness as has not been witnessed since apostolic times. The Spirit and power of God will be poured out upon His children."[1]

What is primitive godliness? It is raw Christianity. It is living by every word that proceeds from the mouth of God. It is loving the Lord our God with all our heart, soul, mind, and strength. It is loving each other as Christ has loved us. It is obeying His commandments and being born again. It is righteousness by faith—confessing with our mouth that Jesus is Lord and believing in our hearts that God has raised Him from the dead. It is recapturing our first love and sharing Him with others. *That* revival of primitive godliness is why we need to pray these prayers.

The second reason for praying prayers of surrender is because Jesus is coming, and we don't want to be swept up in end-time delusions, especially those that may come from within our own hearts. As we learned in the previous chapter, "The human heart is the most deceitful of all things, and desperately wicked. Who really knows how bad it is?" (Jeremiah 17:9, NLT). The first warning Jesus gave the disciples about the end times was, "Watch out that you are not deceived" (Luke 21:8). And it is for that reason we are praying, "Change me" and "Search me"—prayers designed to disturb our comfort zones and awaken us spiritually. That leads us to this chapter's closing prayer: "Lord, wake me."

Spiritual narcolepsy

Narcolepsy is a serious condition. People with this disorder experience excessive sleepiness and can fall asleep in the middle of any activity. You probably don't want an Uber driver with narcolepsy, a narcoleptic dentist during a root canal, a narcoleptic urologist during a vasectomy, or a narcoleptic pilot during the landing of a plane. Preachers don't want narcoleptic members during a sermon. This condition can be dangerous while driving, operating heavy machines, or just before probation closes and Jesus returns to Earth. That's not the time to fake a prayer. That's the time to be wide awake.

> The crisis is stealing gradually upon us. The sun shines in the heavens, passing over its usual round, and the heavens still declare the glory of God. Men are still eating and drinking, planting and building, marrying, and giving in marriage. Merchants are still buying and selling. Men are jostling one against another, contending for the highest place. Pleasure lovers are still crowding to theaters, horse races, gambling hells. The highest excitement prevails, yet probation's hour is fast closing, and every case is about to be eternally decided. Satan sees that his time is short. He has set all his agencies at work that men may be deceived, deluded, occupied and entranced, until the day of probation shall be ended, and the door of mercy be forever shut.
>
> Solemnly there come to us down through the centuries the warning words of our Lord from the Mount of Olives: "Take heed to yourselves, lest at any time your hearts be overcharged with surfeiting, and drunkenness, and cares of this life, and so that day come upon you unawares." "Watch ye therefore, and pray always, that ye may be accounted worthy to escape all these things that shall come to pass, and to stand before the Son of man."[2]

This describes the delusion of normalcy (a.k.a. "the days of Noah") we read about in Matthew 24:37–42. The days of Noah sound a lot like the days of COVID-19, and the warning is to watch out so that the day of Christ's coming doesn't come upon us unawares. (My translation: While we are sleeping! While we are otherwise occupied.) And human beings tend to succumb to spiritual narcolepsy at the worst possible times, as evidenced in the following scene from the life of Jesus.

> Jesus went out as usual to the Mount of Olives, and his disciples followed him. On reaching the place, he said to them, "Pray that you will not fall into temptation." He withdrew about a stone's throw beyond them, knelt down and prayed, "Father, if you are willing, take this cup from me; yet not my will, but yours be done." An angel from heaven appeared to him and strengthened him. And being in anguish, he prayed more earnestly, and his sweat was like drops of blood falling to the ground.
>
> When he rose from prayer and went back to the disciples, he found them asleep, exhausted from sorrow. "Why are you sleeping?" he asked them. "Get up and pray so that you will not fall into temptation" (Luke 22:39–46).

Please note the timing of this incident—just hours before Jesus is to die on the cross and give His life as a ransom for you and for me. The destiny of the human race is hanging in the balance. "For this he [Satan] had been preparing during the three years of Christ's ministry. Everything was at stake with him. If he failed here, his hope of mastery was lost."[3]

Imagine how intently the enemy prepared for this moment! As I write this, two football teams are preparing to face off in the Super Bowl. By the time you read these words, that contest will have been decided, but the following details hold true for any team in a championship game. The entire season comes down to one last sixty-minute battle. All the blood, sweat, and tears to get to this point will culminate in either victory or defeat. Think of the preparation and the hours spent breaking down game film, studying every weakness and strength of the opponent. That's how Satan must have prepared for Gethsemane!

Satan had tried to take out Jesus in His infancy, using Herod's genocide against all the male children two years and under. But he missed, and Jesus escaped into Egypt. Satan tried again in the wilderness immediately following Jesus' baptism. At the time when Jesus was physically at His weakest, Satan appeared as an angel of light and tempted Jesus to give into self-preservation, self-defense, and self-aggrandizement. Though weak physically, His fasting and prayer had strengthened Him spiritually, and Jesus rebuked the enemy three times with the Word of God as His weapon. Another defeat for the once covering cherub.

Again and again, the wicked one took his best shots at destroying the

Son of God, only to be thwarted every time. He tried to drown Jesus in a storm on the Sea of Galilee. Jesus told the winds and the waves to knock it off, and the sea turned to glass. In another storm designed to take the disciples out, Jesus walked on the water! At one point, a mob tried to push Jesus over a cliff, but He passed through their midst unharmed. Nothing that Satan had in his bag of tricks worked—not demons, not praise, not censure, not popularity, not hunger, not thirst, and not sorrow. Now was Satan's last chance. It was the Super Bowl in the plan of redemption, and the enemy and his legions were primed and ready to unleash the last and most powerful temptations against Christ.

Knowing the fierceness of the battle about to be fought, Jesus said to His disciples, "Pray that you will not fall into temptation" (verse 40). But they couldn't do it! Not even for one hour. It's like those times you're watching something really good on TV. You're near the climax of the show, and you know all you have to do is stay awake maybe fifteen minutes more, only to wake up and realize you missed the ending.

And this is what happened to the disciples—not once but three times. Luke only records one of these times in verse 45, but note the reason given for the narcolepsy: "When he rose from prayer and went back to the disciples, he found them asleep, exhausted from sorrow" (verse 45). The last phrase jumped out at me—*exhausted from sorrow.* Here's a true statement: *We are most vulnerable to temptation and sin when we are worn out with worry and grief.* And right now, you should be wide awake to what I'm about to say.

"The age of overwhelm"
Right now, all of us are living in a state of chronic exhaustion—exhaustion not just of body but of mind and spirit. We are worn out from the stress, fear, and disruption of COVID-19; exhausted by masks and the controversy over masks; exhausted by the science and the contradictory reports from the science; exhausted by the politics of the pandemic and the blame and shame associated with it from both sides; exhausted by canceled plans, awkward travel, lack of physical contact, trampled traditions, and the constant state of uncertainty; exhausted by the rising number of cases across the country, the number of deaths, new variants, and fears of loved ones or ourselves contracting the virus.

We live, as a popular book title says, in *The Age of Overwhelm.* In that book, journalist and author Amanda Petrusich is quoted as saying, "These days, people seem to be perpetually gearing themselves up for the epic battle of merely existing. At the end of the day, jogging up to our front doors, we are all Rocky, reaching the summit, conquering that last step: 'Just a man / and his will / to survive!' We rip our headphones off, triumphantly. We did it! Another day closer to death!"[4] It feels that way these days, doesn't it? It's exhausting—and dangerous. And that's why we need to pray the dangerous prayer, "Wake me." It's the wrong time to sleep.

"By these sleeping disciples is represented a sleeping church, when the day of God's visitation is nigh. It is a time of clouds and thick darkness, when to be found asleep is most perilous."[5]

The disciples were exhausted from sorrow. What sorrow were the disciples dealing with? Jesus was the One bearing the cup. But they had heard Jesus talk about one of their own betraying Him (Mark 14:18). They had heard Jesus talk about His impending death, and Peter had said he was ready to die with Him (verses 29–31). They were armed for some kind of conflict, having taken two swords (Luke 22:38). They saw Jesus' demeanor and felt the weight of His burden (Matthew 26:37, 38), and they were sad (Mark 14:19). The combination of all these factors caused adrenal fatigue that left them unable to do the one thing Jesus needed them to do.

We are most vulnerable to temptation and sin when we are worn out with worry and grief.

But exhaustion and sorrow are no excuse for failure to pray. "The church of God is required to fulfill her night watch, however perilous, whether long or short. Sorrow is no excuse for her to be less watchful. Tribulation should not lead to carelessness, but to double vigilance."[6]

Now, in the age of overwhelm, our need to watch and pray that we fall not into temptation is doubled. Earlier, when Jesus had taught His disciples to pray, "Lead us not into temptation" (Matthew 6:13), He was referring to the temptation of choosing our own ways over the ways of God.[7] We are tempted to do the opposite of Proverbs 3:5–7: lean on our own understanding and be wise in our own eyes instead of trusting in the Lord with all our heart.

This was the very temptation Christ was battling in the garden, and it is the very temptation He didn't want the disciples to succumb to. It is also the same temptation we face now and will again tomorrow in these closing hours of Earth's history. Right now, there are those in the church asking, "Is it worth it to do it God's way?" "Is there another less costly option?" This was the last temptation of Christ, and it will be ours also.

The consequences of sleeping instead of praying
"When Jesus' followers saw what was going to happen, they said, 'Lord, should we strike with our swords?' And one of them struck the servant of the high priest, cutting off his right ear" (Luke 22:49, 50).

Wake me, Jesus, because when I sleep, I respond inappropriately in crisis. In Matthew's account, Jesus sought to excuse their weakness by saying, "The spirit is willing, but the flesh is weak" (Matthew 26:41). Having slept, Peter now acts, not according to the Spirit but according to his own weak, unprepared flesh. And there is too much weak, unsanctified flesh on display among the people of God today!

> There is too much weak, unsanctified flesh on display among the people of God today!

Our exhaustion with trying to make America the kingdom of God is killing us. We battle over party and policy with as much vitriol and vinegar as the people of the world. And with our words and tweets, we lash out and cut off ears, thinking we're doing God a favor. But it's the wrong response, and Jesus says, "Put your sword back in its place," "for all who draw the sword will die by the sword" (verse 52).

In the current crisis, we need to know how to respond correctly. Get up and pray so that you will not fall into temptation.

Wake me, Jesus, because when I sleep, I take offense at the ways of God. "The disciples were terrified as they saw Jesus permit Himself to be taken and bound. They were offended that He should suffer this humiliation to Himself and them. They could not understand His conduct, and they blamed Him for submitting to the mob. In their indignation and fear, Peter proposed that they save themselves. Following this suggestion, 'they all forsook Him and fled.' "[8]

Why couldn't they understand what Jesus was doing? Because they had slept when they should have been praying! They had really been sleepwalking since the Passover supper, where they had been arguing about the seating arrangements at the table. *When you sleep instead of praying, you are petty and self-absorbed, and the ways of God offend you.* It doesn't make sense to serve your enemies instead of taking revenge on them, but those who are awake to the Spirit choose the ways of God.

Wake me, Jesus, because when I sleep, I get more distant from the Savior. "Then seizing him, they led him away and took him into the house of the high priest. Peter followed at a distance" (Luke 22:54).

Peter followed at a distance. And *when we sleep instead of praying, our relationship gets distant and strange.* Give Peter some credit, his love for Jesus compelled him to follow, but he did so while trying to blend in with the crowd. What crowds are you blending into? There are so many groups, causes, voices, banners, and flags. Which do you identify with?

Jesus said, "I am coming soon. Hold on to what you have, so that no one will take your crown" (Revelation 3:11). He's saying, "Don't let any man, woman, or philosophy take your crown. Do not lose your identity as a son or daughter of the King in the cacophony of voices shouting for you to identify with them. Know who you are and *whose* you are." In this hour of crisis, stay awake, and get as close to Jesus as you can.

Wake me, Jesus, because when I sleep, I deny You.
And when some there had kindled a fire in the middle of the courtyard and had sat down together, Peter sat down with them. A servant girl saw him seated there in the firelight. She looked closely at him and said, "This man was with him."

But he denied it. "Woman, I don't know him," he said.

A little later someone else saw him and said, "You also are one of them."

"Man, I am not!" Peter replied.

About an hour later another asserted, "Certainly this fellow was with him, for he is a Galilean."

Peter replied, "Man, I don't know what you're talking about!" Just as he was speaking, the rooster crowed. The Lord turned and looked straight at Peter. Then Peter remembered the word the Lord had spoken to him: "Before the rooster crows today, you will disown me three times." And he went outside and wept bitterly (Luke 22:55–62).

For every time Peter slept when encouraged by Jesus to pray, he denied Him. Our danger is that if we sleep now, we, too, could end up denying our Lord. Be careful with your thoughts, words, and actions during this time of exhaustion and overwhelm. When we trust ourselves and lash out in condemnation or judgment against a brother or sister with whom we disagree, we are declaring, as Peter did, "I don't know the Man!"

Peter thought he knew himself. He thought he knew what was in his heart and had boasted, "Even if all fall away, I will not" (Mark 14:29). But he trusted in himself. And this is our greatest temptation in the last days—to trust in ourselves (our good works, our experience, our knowledge, etc.). Our only safety is to pray, "Search me, O God, and wake me."

"Remaining Awake Through a Great Revolution"
Just four days before his assassination at the hands of James Earl Ray in a Memphis motel, Martin Luther King Jr. gave his final Sunday sermon at the National Cathedral in Washington, DC. In that historic house of worship, the message that was heavy on his heart was titled "Remaining Awake Through a Great Revolution."

With that rich and melodic voice that had given unparalleled inspiration to the civil rights revolution, Dr. King recounted the story of Rip Van Winkle, who famously slept for twenty years. The twenty-year nap is what most people remember about Washington Irving's fantastic tale. But an often-overlooked detail was what Dr. King wanted to focus on. That detail was a picture of King George III of England that hung on the wall of a little inn in the town from which Rip went up into the mountains for his long sleep. Twenty years later, Rip returned to that same inn, but the picture on the wall had changed. Another George was there—George Washington, the first president of the United States. At the beginning of his sleep, America was still under British rule. When he awakened, America was a free and independent nation.

"And this reveals to us that the most striking thing about the story of Rip Van Winkle is not merely that Rip slept twenty years," Dr. King stated, "but that he slept through a revolution. While he was peacefully snoring up in the mountain, a revolution was taking place that at points would change the course of history—and Rip knew nothing about it. He was asleep. Yes, he slept through a revolution."[9]

I agree with Dr. King that there is nothing more tragic than sleeping through a revolution. In 1968, there were too many Rip Van Winkles sleeping through a revolution—living at an unprecedented time of great social change yet unable to develop the new attitudes, mental responses, and behaviors to meet the demands of that change.

And what about today? Is the church of God the new Rip Van Winkle of the twenty-first century, sleeping through a time of great social, political, technological, and spiritual change? Why do we insist on clinging to the same old things when God wants to do a new thing?

A pastor friend shared an anonymous Facebook post he saw at the end of 2020. The person posting asked for others to join him in praying for the new year.

> Yes, that COVID will leave us alone, yes that some consistent pattern will return to our lives, but more than these: pray that we won't go back to normal! Normal was killing the church in North America. Normal got us to a place where 87% of our churches are either plateaued or dying. Normal got us to a place where we are shutting down Adventist schools all over the division. Normal helped us reach a statistic of nearly equal the number of former Adventists in our division as we have on our member roles [*sic*]. Normal helped us fall from an average of 50% in attendance on a Sabbath morning to 30% in the last five years. Normal looks like 10% of the people doing 100% of the work. Normal meant 7 in 10 of our young people will leave this community of faith by their second year of college. Normal is almost nonexistent discipleship. Normal is no good! So pray Jesus doesn't let us personally or corporately go back to normal ever again!

There's a revolution going on—not in the streets but in the "heavenlies." It is the "time of the latter rain" (Zechariah 10:1, KJV), and the spiritual refreshing is freely available to all who are awake enough to ask for it. "Do you not perceive it?" (Isaiah 43:19).

"There are some who, instead of wisely improving present opportunities, are idly waiting for some special season of spiritual refreshing by which their ability to enlighten others will be greatly increased. They neglect present duties and privileges, and allow their light to burn dim, while they look forward to a time when, without any effort on their part, they will be made the recipients of special blessing, by which they will be transformed and fitted for service."[10]

There is nothing more tragic than sleeping through a revolution.

This is a tragic mistake. If we would remain awake through God's great revolution, we must not wait for a more opportune time to improve our present opportunities and pray for rain. The time is now!

The disciples slept through the moment of the greatest battle for the souls of humanity just before the death of Jesus. We modern disciples must not sleep through this moment of great revival just before the triumphant return of Jesus. This is the wrong time to sleep through a revolution.

Everything in the world is in agitation. The signs of the times are ominous. Coming events cast their shadows before. The Spirit of God is withdrawing from the earth, and calamity follows calamity by sea and by land. There are tempests, earthquakes, fires, floods, murders of every grade. Who can read the future? Where is security? There is assurance in nothing that is human or earthly. Rapidly are men ranging themselves under the banner they have chosen. Restlessly are they waiting and watching the movements of their leaders. There are those who are waiting and watching and working for our Lord's appearing. Another class are falling into line under the generalship of the first great apostate. Few believe with heart and soul that we have a hell to shun and a heaven to win.[11]

In what areas of your life are you spiritually asleep? Where in your life is the spirit willing but the flesh weak? Use the prayer space below to journal your answers and submit them to God.

> "Wake up, sleeper,
> rise from the dead,
> and Christ will shine on you."

Be very careful, then, how you live—not as unwise but as wise, making the most of every opportunity, because the days are evil (Ephesians 5:14–16).

Make the most of this and every opportunity.
Get up and pray so that you will not fall into temptation.

Closing Prayer

Father God, wake me out of my spiritual stupor. Now is not the time for sleep. Not now. Not this close to the end of all things. I confess my exhaustion to You, Lord. I am overwhelmed with sorrow over the sin I still see in my own life as well as the sin I see in the world around me. The darkness is deep and thick and threatens to swallow the little faith I have. Awaken me to those areas in my life where I am choosing my way over Yours, where I am responding inappropriately in crises, where I am leaning on my own understanding and allowing my relationship with You to become distant and strange. Open my eyes to see where the spirit is willing, but my flesh is weak. Don't let me sleep through a revolution and deny You, Lord. And thank You for never giving up on me. Amen.

My Closing Prayer

Write yours here: _______________________________________

---

1. Ellen G. White, *The Great Controversy* (Mountain View, CA: Pacific Press®, 1950), 464.

2. Ellen G. White, *The Desire of Ages* (Mountain View, CA: Pacific Press®, 1940), 636.

3. White, 687.

4. Amanda Petrusich, quoted in Laura van Dernoot Lipsky, *The Age of Overwhelm* (Oakland, CA: Berrett-Koehler, 2018), 13, https://www.readpbn.com/pdf/The-Age-of -Overwhelm-Sample-Pages.pdf.

5. Ellen G. White, *Testimonies for the Church* (Mountain View, CA: Pacific Press®, 1948), 2:205.

6. White, 2:205.

7. See Francis D. Nichol, ed., *The Seventh-day Adventist Bible Commentary* (Washington, DC: Review and Herald®, 1980), 5:348.

8. White, *Desire of Ages*, 697.

9. Pax Aeterna, "The Last Sunday Sermon of Rev. Dr. Martin Luther King Jr.," sermon by Martin Luther King Jr., March 31, 1968, video, 47:26, August 18, 2019, https://www .youtube.com/watch?v=uFmP3YA3i9g.

10. Ellen G. White, *The Acts of the Apostles* (Mountain View, CA: Pacific Press®, 1911), 54.

11. White, *Desire of Ages*, 636.

4

BREAK ME

My sacrifice, O God, is a broken spirit;
a broken and contrite heart
you, God, will not despise.
　　　　　　　　　　　　　　　　—Psalm 51:17

We must never choose the scene of our own martyrdom.
If ever we are going to be made into wine,
we will have to be crushed; you cannot drink grapes.
Grapes become wine only when they have been squeezed.
　　　　　　　　　　　　　　　　—Oswald Chambers

I was twelve years old when I nearly fell off a mountain.

OK, that was a bit dramatic. To be more precise, I slid down a hillside, which, for an adolescent city kid who was experiencing his first or second summer camp in the mountains, *was* pretty dramatic.

The trouble started when Kevin, my best friend, cracked a joke that made me laugh and lose my footing on the narrow mountain trail we were walking along. The hillside below the trail sloped away at a steep angle, and I began to tumble and slide down at a pretty fast clip. The drama of the situation was heightened by the fact that at the bottom of the hill was a river that ran through the camp. It was a river that you could hear from all over the camp but was hard to see through the trees from most spots above it. As I slid, I feared it would be mere seconds before I was not only going to see the river but be in it. In desperation, I tried my best to grab onto anything that would slow my momentum—rocks, twigs, dirt—anything. Suddenly, out of nowhere, my flailing hands found the root of a tree sticking up out of the ground. Surely the Lord must have planted it there just for me! I grabbed onto that root like a drowning person grabs onto a life preserver, and it held fast, breaking my fall and stopping me from taking a swim that day.

That true story helps me identify somewhat with the hiker in this fictional one: A man slipped and fell off a cliff while hiking on a mountaintop. Luckily, he was able to grab a branch on his way down. Holding on for dear life, he looked down to see a rock valley some fifteen hundred feet below. When he looked up, it was twenty feet to the cliff where he had fallen.

Panicked, he yelled, "Help! Somebody, save me!"

A booming voice spoke up. "I am here, and I will save you *if* you trust me."

"I trust you! I trust you!" yelled back the man.

"If you trust me, then you must do what I tell you to do."

"Yes, I trust you! I'll do what you tell me to do!"

"All right," the voice commanded, "let go of the branch."

The young man looks up, then looks back down, then looks back up again, and shouts, "Is there *anybody else* up there?"

Out on a limb

Out on a limb—that's how I feel as I approach this chapter. It's like hanging onto that branch and having your rescuer tell you, "Let me break that off for you." I can't speak for you, but I'd be swinging my legs and trying to kick that nut away from my branch. You too? Thought so. But what if breaking the branch was the only way to get off that mountain? What if breaking *you* is the only way to save you?

If the closing prayers "Search me" and "Wake me" are challenging (and they are!), then praying, "Lord, break me," takes it to a whole other level. But remember why we are praying these closing prayers in the first place: to clear the way for revival and to avoid end-time delusions—especially those that may come from within our own hearts.

Suffice it to say, this is a prayer nobody wants to pray, including me! When I started reading Craig Groeschel's book, and I got to that section, I wanted to skip over it. Like surgery, just put me to sleep and wake me when it's over. But it reminded me of something I know is true, and I've said it many times: *there can be no Pentecost without Calvary!*

An uneasy fireside chat

In his book, Craig writes about a small group meeting he and his wife hosted with seven or eight other couples on a cold night in January. While it was probably fifteen degrees outside, they were cozy and warm inside, sitting around a warm fire, having filled their stomachs with homemade chili and corn bread. It was in that setting they discussed the dangerous prayer "Break me." The living room was cozy; the conversation was not.

One lady said, "Sorry, but I've got to be honest. I don't want to ask God to break me. I'm afraid of what will happen. I'm a mom with four kids. I love them too much. Asking God to break me is simply too scary for me to ever pray. What if I get sick or depressed or pulled away from my family?"

Most other people in the small group nodded in agreement. One by one, each person explained why they were hesitant, afraid, and unwilling to pray that dangerous prayer. So we continued talking about it, each of us identifying and justifying why it was okay not to pray such a dangerous prayer. All of us Christians, lounging comfortably near the fire, sipping on warm coffee with soft praise music playing in the background.

At the end of our time together, though no one prayed it out loud, the cry of our hearts seemed clear: "Keep us comfortable, God. Keep us warm and cozy. Don't break us—it would hurt too much. Please, just keep things going smoothly."[1]

The author then asks these questions: "What are we losing by clinging to our comfort? What are we missing out on because we're so committed to avoiding pain and discomfort?"[2]

Too many are in the church but not in the faith.

Whether we care to admit it or not, COVID is breaking us. The invisible enemy has cracked our psyches in ways we couldn't have imagined when the pandemic first reached America. It, along with other comfort-breaking events since then, have exposed cracks in our Christianity as troublesome as those discovered on the West Seattle Bridge, near where I live. And before that bridge will be useful again, it will have to be broken and rebuilt.

Breaking down to break through

"Examine yourselves," Paul said, "to see whether you are in the faith" (2 Corinthians 13:5). Search me, wake me, break me. Why? Because *too many are in the church but not in the faith*. While we shake our heads in perplexity, wondering why God does not move in revival power on the church, to quote Leonard Ravenhill, "He is wondering why we do not break! We wish He would bend low; He wishes we would break down."[3]

In the churches I've pastored, it's been my practice to choose a word or phrase that will serve as our guiding theme for the new year. In 2020, the word of the challenge was *breakthrough*. One of our elders sent me a video that metaphorically pictured the new year as flight 2020, with Captain

Emmanuel thanking us for choosing Salvation Airline.

"Flight 2020 will be taking off from January airport to December airport," the narrator began. "Please be reminded that during our flight, we will land in 12 interesting sites taking us to a total of 365 amazing days."[4] It was cute and filled with the hope every new year brings. Little did we know then that we'd only get to the third of those twelve "sites" before the pandemic bomb exploded, and we've been trying to avoid crashing ever since!

But we were blissfully ignorant then. All we wanted was to break through in our devotion to God, to break through the status quo, and reach for the new thing God had for us in 2020.

We didn't want to be satisfied, but we may have underestimated what a breakthrough requires. *Just like there can be no Pentecost without Calvary, there can be no breakthrough without a breakdown.* A breakthrough begins at the altar of brokenness. And what's on the altar is me and my raging love of self.

The prophet Joel gives us a picture of what the revival of primitive godliness looks like:

> "And afterward,
>   I will pour out my Spirit on all people.
> Your sons and daughters will prophesy,
>   your old men will dream dreams,
>   your young men will see visions.
> Even on my servants, both men and women,
>   I will pour out my Spirit in those days" (Joel 2:28, 29).

Don't you long to see this with your own eyes—the Lord moving in power among His people? A return of the glory of His presence and His wonders! This is the breakthrough we seek.

But we cannot ignore the means God requires of us to secure the blessing. What are those means? Brokenness. Notice the revival promise begins with the words "And afterward . . ." After what? Something obviously came before the breakthrough—before the Lord pours His Spirit on all people. Back up and look at verses 12–17 for the answer:

"Even now," declares the Lord,
   "*return* to me with all your heart,
   with fasting and weeping and mourning."

Rend your heart
   and not your garments.
Return to the Lord your God,
   for he is gracious and compassionate,
slow to anger and abounding in love,
   and he relents from sending calamity. . . .

Blow the trumpet in Zion,
   declare a holy fast,
   call a sacred assembly.
Gather the people,
   consecrate the assembly;
bring together the elders,
   gather the children,
   those nursing at the breast.
Let the bridegroom leave his room
   and the bride her chamber.
Let the priests, who minister before the Lord,
   weep between the portico and the altar.
Let them say, "Spare your people, Lord.
   Do not make your inheritance an object of scorn,
   a byword among the nations.
Why should they say among the peoples,
   'Where is their God?' " (verses 12, 13, 15–17; emphasis added).

There it is! The cause that produced the effect of revival in verses 28 and 29. It is a call to return to God with all our hearts. A call to self-denial. A call to repentance. A call to anguish. Why anguish? Isn't that a little too intense? It depends on how much you care.

In a sermon preached by the late David Wilkerson, the founder of Teen Challenge and the author of *The Cross and the Switchblade,* he asked,

Whatever happened to anguish in the house of God? Whatever happened to anguish in the ministry? It's a word you don't hear in this pampered age. You don't hear it. Anguish means extreme pain and distress. The emotions so stirred that it becomes painful. Acute, deeply felt inner pain because of conditions about you, in you, or around you. . . . We've held on to our religious rhetoric, and our revival talk, but we've become so passive. . . .

I know now it will take more than preaching. More than a new revelation. There's going to be no renewal, no revival, no awakening until we are willing to let Him once again break us.[5]

I listened to the sermon again this week, and I had to pray because it's hard to hear. But I know it's true. *Awakenings are preceded by breakings,* but we haven't been that concerned. More of us are in anguish over the state of the economy or who's in the White House than we are over the state of the church or the state of our hearts.

Comfort cannot continue to be our first priority. Our buildings, our programs, our services and religious rituals, and our rhetoric—none of these impresses God. What does impress Him? Our key text says it: "My sacrifice, O God, is a broken spirit; a broken and contrite heart you, God, will not despise" (Psalm 51:17).

Three examples of brokenness

We can learn a lot about what it means to be broken from three examples in Scripture: David, the Last Supper, and the woman who anointed Jesus.

Psalm 51 is a psalm of David after Nathan confronted him about his sin with Bathsheba. His song of repentance helps us understand brokenness. "Against you, you only, have I sinned and done what is evil in your sight" (verse 4). *To pray "Lord, break me" is to get real about sin.* David's sin was not just against Bathsheba and Uriah. It was against God. To pray "Lord, break me" is to own our sin. No blaming others or pointing fingers. David says, "Blot out my transgressions. Wash away all my iniquity and cleanse me from my sin" (verses 1, 2).

A key to brokenness is humility—something sorely lacking in the socio-political discourse of our day. David's sin was birthed from his own ego. There he was, the king of Israel. He should have been on the battlefield fighting because it was springtime—the time when kings go off to war.

But David decided to sit this one out, and while bored one day in the palace, he went out onto his rooftop terrace and spotted a beautiful woman bathing. Too bad there wasn't an angel linebacker to take David down to the ground right then, like the Houston-area mother who tackled a man she caught peeking in her daughter's bedroom window. The suspect was able to give two officers the slip, but Phyllis Pena wasn't having it. With a police dashcam rolling, the video captures Phyllis making an open-field tackle on the fleeing peeper, which would have made any pro linebacker proud.[6] But there was no Phyllis Pena on the terrace that day to stop the Lord's anointed peeper.

David was full of himself and filled with lust for the woman and had her brought to the palace. He slept with another man's wife and hatched a murderous plot to cover up his sin. David lost the touch of humility in his life and became a law unto himself. *If you will not be broken before God, it is inevitable that you will break the law and the heart of God.* In order for God to use any of us, self has got to go. God has to break us of pride, self-confidence, self-sufficiency, and even of some things we don't know that need to be removed from our lives.

Peter didn't know what was in his heart when he told Jesus, "Even if all fall away on account of you, I never will" (Matthew 26:33). He was absolutely sincere when he said those words. But Peter didn't know himself as Jesus did. He didn't know what lurked in his own heart.

And that's why David prayed,

> You desired faithfulness even in the womb;
>   you taught me wisdom in that secret place. . . .
> Create in me a pure heart, O God,
>   and renew a steadfast spirit within me (Psalm 51:6, 10).

No surface praying! David knows his issues run deep, so he asks for a deep working of the Holy Spirit to re-create his heart. Are our prayers in these closing hours going deep enough?

I wonder because during the early months of the COVID-19 outbreak, when there was so much fear and uncertainty, I noticed, as I'm sure you did, a conspicuous increase in calls for prayer. In the Washington Conference, where I currently serve as prayer coordinator, we held a "Faith Over Fear" prayer call every Sabbath afternoon for a month. There were multiple virtual prayer rallies and days of prayer. Everybody was praying as the virus and the racial-reckoning protests, sparked by the George Floyd and Breonna Taylor killings, appeared to be ushering us into the apocalypse.

But the one thing conspicuous by its absence in many of the calls for prayer around the nation was repentance. Prayers for deliverance? Yes. Prayers for protection? Abundant. Prayers for God's mercy and justice? Of course. But prayers of penitence? Of brokenness? Was there an "against you, you only, have I sinned and done what is evil in your sight" prayer in the house? These days it's much easier to boil over than to break down.

Broken and poured out

The second example of what it means to be broken comes from the night Jesus broke bread at the Last Supper. Luke 22:19 says, "And he took bread, gave thanks and broke it, and gave it to them, saying, 'This is my body given for you; do this in remembrance of me.' " Some scholars believe "do this" refers to more than the ritual of Communion. Some believe this also refers to how we are to live. "We don't just remember Jesus during Holy Communion at church; we remember him in how we live our lives daily. Because Jesus' body was broken, because his blood was poured out for us, we too should live daily for him, broken and poured out."[7] It is the way of Christ's followers. Because our Savior lived a broken and poured-out life, we who follow Him are expected to live broken and poured-out lives.

Oswald Chambers, in *My Utmost for His Highest*, says that God calls us to be made broken bread and poured-out wine.

God can never make us wine if we object to the fingers He uses to crush us with. If God would only use His own fingers and make me broken bread and poured-out wine in a special way! But when He uses someone whom we dislike, or some set of circumstances to which we said we would never submit, and makes those the crushers, we object. We must never choose the scene of our own martyrdom. If ever we are going to be made into wine, we will have to be crushed; you cannot drink grapes. Grapes become wine only when they have been squeezed.[8]

Recent events have been squeezing the wine out of all of us and what is coming out of too many is remarkably bitter! "Keep right with God," Oswald finishes, "and let Him do what He likes, and you will find that He is producing the kind of bread and wine that will benefit His other children."[9] When we are broken, we can bless.

All of me

Our final example of brokenness is the woman who anointed Jesus. John identifies the woman as Mary of Bethany, a.k.a. Mary of Magdala—a former prostitute out of whom Jesus cast seven demons. The other Gospels don't name her, but the dinner is held in Jesus' honor at the house of Simon the leper.

Into this scene, where Jesus is seated at the place of honor (the resurrected Lazarus on his left and the restored Simon on his right), comes this woman with a reputation and this woman with a past. Mary was also a woman to whom Jesus had shown unconditional love. He treated her with dignity and respect, honoring her when others had treated her with contempt and as an object to be used. And she wanted to show her gratitude before Jesus' death.

In an act of unrestrained worship and devotion, Mary "came with an alabaster jar of very expensive perfume, made of pure nard. She broke the jar and poured the perfume on his head" (Mark 14:3). Then she wet His feet with her tears and wiped them with her hair. It was an act of supreme worship. Though the perfume represented a year's wages, she broke the bank and gave it all to Jesus.

Most women in those days did not wear perfume. It was too expensive. Because it was so costly, only prostitutes and the wealthy could afford it. The women of the street would use it as advertising to let men know they were available. The fact that Mary had the perfume in a bottle and was not wearing it testified to the deliverance Jesus had worked in her life. She was no longer turning tricks because, in turning her eyes upon Jesus, she had turned from her wicked ways.

With the breaking of that bottle, all bridges were burned—no going back. Mary poured out all the contents on Jesus, symbolizing that she would give Him all of her life. *To pray "Lord, break me" is to say, "Lord, take all of me."* I'm holding nothing back. You can have it all. She, who was broken in sin and was willing to break with her past, gave her all to the One who put her back together again. Has Jesus put you back together again? That depends on whether a breaking has taken place. You'll never give your all if you don't realize how broken you are and how much you need Him to heal you. You'll hold onto your alabaster jar, and Jesus won't be honored in your life. Why? Because what is unbroken remains shut up to itself, sealed in its container—like Simon.

Simon was offended by Mary's brokenness and unrestrained devotion. He questioned whether Jesus was a prophet because He allowed this sinful woman to touch Him in such an intimate and vulgar manner. Healed he was. Broken he was not. Consequently, Simon could be a blessing to no one, including the Savior.

> It was Simon's ignorance of God and of Christ that led him to think as he did. He did not realize that God's Son must act in God's way, with compassion, tenderness, and mercy. . . .
>
> Simon's coldness and neglect toward the Saviour showed how little he appreciated the mercy he had received. . . . While Mary was a sinner pardoned, he was a sinner unpardoned.[10]

And unbroken people never appreciate the aroma of forgiveness.

There must be a breaking in order to benefit from and enjoy what's inside. When Mary broke the seal on that jar, the aroma of the perfume filled the whole house. Everyone knew what had happened because of the smell that was in the air. It was the smell of devotion.

But when life and stress break us, what is the aroma that comes out? Is it a sweet-smelling fragrance to God, or is it the stench of bitterness, criticism, faultfinding, and rage?

There is a breaking happening to the church right now! The trauma "lasagna," with its layers that we're all ingesting, is a breaking, and we must understand how to benefit and bless the world with what's inside.

This is the moment that the world has been waiting for. It is also the moment God has been waiting for. In the breaking, will God's people fill their homes and communities with the aroma of Jesus? What does the world smell from God's people who are being broken at this closing hour of Earth's history? Before Jesus comes back, He is looking for a group of people who will not only keep the commandments of God but have the faith of Jesus—a people who will give their all and worship Him fully.

We are broken to worship fully; we are broken to serve freely; we are broken to repent deeply and humbly. Are we ready to pray this prayer? Am I? I don't want to be like Peter and say, "Even if no one else breaks, I will!" I don't want to hear any roosters crowing! I admit that I am a coward and don't know myself. But I know enough to know I need help, and the prayer I will pray is "Lord, help me!" Will you join me in that prayer? It's kind of like falling off a mountain. But God will be there to catch us.

Closing Prayer

Father, this is the scariest prayer of all. I want my life to be filled with the sweet aroma of Christ, but I smell too much of self. You know what to do, Lord. I do not. Help me. That's all I have the courage to say. But do not leave me shut up to myself, deceived and unrepentant. Let me live a life that is broken and spilled out for You.

My Closing Prayer

Write yours here: ____

____

____

____

____

---

1. Craig Groeschel, *Dangerous Prayers* (Grand Rapids, MI: Zondervan, 2020), 72.

2. Groeschel, 72.

3. Leonard Ravenhill, *Revival Praying: An Urgent and Powerful Message for the Family of Christ* (n.p.: n.p., 2016), 89, Kindle.

4. Keith Ngesi Media, "Flight With Salvation Airlines Into 2020 With Captain Emmanuel (GOD Is With Us)," Facebook video, January 23, 2020, posted by Jesus Generation Ministry's [*sic*], https://fb.watch/v/9WxyIig77/.

5. Back2Truch.cu.cc, "A Call to Anguish – David Wilkerson (Extended)," sermon by David Wilkerson, February 7, 2014, video, 11:51, https://youtu.be/QcUh2xLmJy4.

6. KPRC 2 Click2Houston, "Mom Tackles Man Suspected of Peeking in Daughter's Window," February 10, 2021, video, 2:05, https://youtu.be/8AsTruj2jVI.

7. Groeschel, *Dangerous Prayers*, 83.

8. Oswald Chambers, *My Utmost for His Highest* (Grand Rapids, MI: Discovery House, 1963), 202 (September 30).

9. Chambers, 202.

10. Ellen G. White, *The Desire of Ages* (Mountain View, CA: Pacific Press®, 1940), 566, 567.

5

SEND ME

*Then I heard the voice of the Lord saying,
"Whom shall I send? And who will go for us?"
And I said, "Here am I. Send me!"*
—Isaiah 6:8

*What if instead of always asking God to do something on
our behalf, we dared to ask God to use us on His behalf?*
—Craig Groeschel

For the last several chapters, we have engaged in a study of closing prayers—prayers that threaten our comfort, the status quo, and Laodicean lukewarmness. To "Change Me," the prayers we have looked at so far are "Search Me," "Wake Me," and "Break Me."

But if all you've done is look at these prayers and not actually prayed them, chances are you are still at peace in Laodicea. It's likely that your status is still quo and that comfort is still king in your life and experience. Your prayers (the nonthreatening variety) most likely echo the sentiments expressed in this fictional marriage proposal to God by Morris Venden, which I included in my book *Bring Back the Glory*:

I am asking You to be my God. However, there are certain qualifications. First, I wish it understood that I love myself more than I do You. My family and friends are also more important to me, which is understandable, I am sure, when You consider that I have known them so much longer than I have You.

Second, if it comes to a crisis with respect to any basic decision, of course, I will consult my own wishes rather than Yours. Some of Your ideas seem very strange to me, and if I am to make a name for myself in the business in which I am employed, I cannot be tied down to Your set of values. I'm sure You understand how I feel.

Third, I am reserving my right to my own time. I am a very busy person and cannot be expected to spend time in communion with You day by day. Whatever time I have left over from my business must be primarily spent with my family and friends.

Fourth, a word about my property. You must understand that it belongs to me exclusively. I find it hard to say goodbye to my money. You own the cattle upon a thousand hills, as well as extensive mining assets, so I can see no reason for You to make any claims on my property or money.

Oh yes, another thing. I cannot bear sickness, tears, or sorrow. So please do not expect me to enter into fellowship with You in suffering. I have no desire to become involved in service to others. Bear Your own cross, and leave me out of it.

However, I do want You to be my God. As such, You will have the full responsibility for providing me with salvation, for showering me with blessings, and for answering my prayers. This will free me to give full attention to myself, my family and friends, my possessions, and my business.

Under the above conditions, I could enjoy having You as my God, and I feel sure we could have some nice times together—maybe on weekends, if I'm not too tired. Will You say Yes? If You do, please begin construction at once on my heavenly mansion. And go ahead with preparation for the marriage supper of the Lamb. I'll plan to be there—if I'm not too busy.[1]

No one in their right minds would ever accept such a proposal, let alone God. But this is what you get when you aren't asking God for changing through searching, waking, and breaking. These are serious times, and they are about to get even more serious. Therefore, we need to take our marriage to God seriously, beginning with the serious prayer:

Search me, God, and know my heart;
    test me and know my anxious thoughts.
See if there is any offensive way in me,
    and lead me in the way everlasting (Psalm 139:23, 24).

This proposal calls for an internal four-level examination of our (1) heart, (2) fears, (3) sin, and (4) leading.

The second serious prayer was "Wake Me." Because we are most vulnerable to temptation and sin when we are worn out with worry and grief, we cannot afford to sleep spiritually right now. Now, when we are worn out over the pandemic and politics, hear Jesus' plea to His disciples in the garden: "Pray that you will not fall into temptation" (Luke 22:40). And the greatest temptations we could fall into are adopting ways and methods of our own choosing, responding inappropriately in crises, taking offense at the ways of God, becoming petty and self-absorbed, getting distant in our relationship with the Savior, and ultimately, denying Christ.

The third prayer was "Break Me." Why this? *Just like there can be no Pentecost without Calvary, there can be no breakthrough without a breakdown.* A breakthrough begins at the altar of brokenness. Awakenings are preceded by breakings: "My sacrifice, O God, is a broken spirit; a broken and contrite heart you, God, will not despise" (Psalm 51:17).

Before you're ready to be sent by God, you must see Him first.

We are broken to worship fully; we are broken to serve freely; we are broken to repent deeply and humbly. True brokenness before God isn't a one-time event. It's a daily choice to die to selfish pride and live as broken bread and poured-out wine to bless others.

This is where we've been, and frankly, we need to put these prayers on repeat and pray them again and again because we are dust (clay); a potter will tell you that clay has a memory. You have to teach the clay to forget what it was in order to make something new out of it. God is shaping us for eternity, not time. And the remaking process is incomplete without this closing prayer: "Send Me."

Once the clay has been searched, awakened, and broken, it is ready to be used. In his book *Dangerous Prayers*, Craig Groeschel asks, "What if instead of always asking God to do something on our behalf, we dared to ask God to use us on His behalf?"[2] To pray "Lord, send me" is to say, "Lord, use me." And that's the prayer of Isaiah that we will consider now. Turn to Isaiah 6.

"In the year that King Uzziah died, I saw the Lord, high and exalted, seated on a throne; and the train of his robe filled the temple" (Isaiah 6:1). Don't miss this: *before you're ready to be sent by God, you must see Him first.* You've got to have your vision corrected.

As chapter 6 opens, Isaiah is visiting the temple. His mind was filled with dread over the sins of his people and the judgments that were sure to fall. He was vulnerable because, like the disciples and us, he was exhausted with worry and grief. After a fifty-two-year reign, Judah's beloved king was dead. Because of their sins, the people of Judah had forfeited divine protection from their enemies. Assyria appeared invincible; it seemed to be only a matter of time before the people of Judah would be overwhelmed, and Assyria would control the world. Isaiah was losing heart. He was on the verge of giving up.

It was a time of uncertainty, desperation, and fear, not unlike now.

But God wanted Isaiah to see more than what he was looking at around him. Sometimes when we're going through stuff, all we can see is the stuff! We can't see the forest for the trees. Nothing makes sense, and we feel lost.

It didn't matter that an earthly king was absent from a temporal throne because the King of kings was still seated on His.

In the time of the prophet Elisha, all that his servant could see on that morning in Dothan was impending doom. "When the servant of the man of God got up and went out early the next morning, an army with horses and chariots had surrounded the city. 'Oh no, my lord, what shall we do?' the servant asked" (2 Kings 6:15). The army of Aram had surrounded the city with a massive show of force. But Elisha wanted his servant to see more than what he was looking at around him.

"Don't be afraid," the prophet answered. "Those who are with us are more than those who are with them."

And Elisha prayed, "Open his eyes, Lord, so that he may see." Then the Lord opened the servant's eyes, and he looked and saw the hills full of horses and chariots of fire all around Elisha (verses 16, 17).

Before, all the servant could see was doom. But after his eyes were opened, all he could see was God's deliverance. God had them surrounded, and no matter what you're going through or the anxieties you come to these pages with today, He's got you surrounded too. There's no way you can lose! But you must have your vision right.

God had opened Isaiah's eyes, too, and allowed the worried prophet to see directly into the throne room of the universe. Isaiah saw the Lord seated on His throne. Instantly, *it didn't matter that an earthly king was absent from a temporal throne because the King of kings was still seated on His.* Changes in government, shifts in the balance of power on Earth, and shake-ups in earthly systems do nothing to shake, shift, or disturb the kingdom of heaven. God is in control. He's not looking down at our government, wringing His hands in a panic, saying, "What are We going to do? This is terrible!" God rules the affairs of men and is in ultimate control of everything concerning us. Therefore, do not be afraid. "The LORD is in his holy temple; let all the earth be silent before him" (Habakkuk 2:20).

When Isaiah was allowed to look into the heavenly temple, he saw three things: (1) God's holiness, (2) his own sinfulness, and (3) God's forgiveness. In God's presence, Isaiah's heart was exposed. He was awakened to his true condition and that of his people, and he was broken in humility. We don't know whether he prayed these dangerous prayers, but he experienced their results all at once because he saw the Lord.

God's holiness

Above him were seraphim, each with six wings: With two wings they covered their faces, with two they covered their feet, and with two they were flying. And they were calling to one another:

> "Holy, holy, holy is the LORD Almighty;
> the whole earth is full of his glory."

At the sound of their voices the doorposts and thresholds shook and the temple was filled with smoke (Isaiah 6:2–4).

The outstanding attribute of God that impresses the angels and calls forth their praise in solemn repetition is His perfect holiness of character. The Hebrew word is *qadosh,* meaning "separate, set apart, morally blameless, physically pure." So holy is God that mortal man cannot look upon Him in His purest essence and live. *And yet Isaiah is seeing Him!* (At least, through the smoke!)

Only a handful of humans have seen what Isaiah saw that day—John the apostle being among them. His detailed description of the heavenly throne room helps our tiny minds to somewhat comprehend the awesome majesty that surrounds the Almighty.

> At once I was in the Spirit, and there before me was a throne in heaven with someone sitting on it. And the one who sat there had

the appearance of jasper and ruby. A rainbow that shone like an emerald encircled the throne. Surrounding the throne were twenty-four other thrones, and seated on them were twenty-four elders. They were dressed in white and had crowns of gold on their heads. From the throne came flashes of lightning, rumblings and peals of thunder. In front of the throne, seven lamps were blazing. These are the seven spirits of God. Also in front of the throne there was what looked like a sea of glass, clear as crystal.

In the center, around the throne, were four living creatures, and they were covered with eyes, in front and in back. The first living creature was like a lion, the second was like an ox, the third had a face like a man, the fourth was like a flying eagle. Each of the four living creatures had six wings and was covered with eyes all around, even under its wings. Day and night they never stop saying:

> "Holy, holy, holy
> is the Lord God Almighty,
> who was, and is, and is to come."

Whenever the living creatures give glory, honor and thanks to him who sits on the throne and who lives for ever and ever, the twenty-four elders fall down before him who sits on the throne and worship him who lives for ever and ever. They lay their crowns before the throne and say:

> "You are worthy, our Lord and God,
>   to receive glory and honor and power,
> for you created all things,
>   and by your will they were created
>   and have their being" (Revelation 4:2–11).

What words can describe our awesome God!? Words fail. The six-winged seraphim are known as the "burning ones." They have the appearance of fire because they are in the immediate presence of the Almighty, whose holiness is "a consuming fire" (Hebrews 12:29). These "burning ones," who cover their faces and feet as they fly, declare, "The whole earth is full of his glory!" (Isaiah 6:3). And this praise goes on 24/7, regardless of what is happening here on this planet.

Why does that matter? Remember, just moments before this vision, Isaiah was depressed. Isaiah was discouraged. The king was dead, and Assyria was on the rise. The fate of his nation was uncertain. Why shouldn't Isaiah be depressed? Because of what the angels are saying: "The whole earth is full of his glory!" No matter how bad things look here, no matter how dark and confused and perplexing our lives may be, the truth is *the whole earth is full of God's glory.*

In a moment, in the twinkling of an eye, Isaiah's perspective is changed as he sees what really is beyond the veil of our human senses. God is in control. The glory of His character and presence, though unseen and unappreciated by sinful beings, is nevertheless everywhere at all times and in all circumstances—including Isaiah's. That change in perspective immediately awakens him to another reality.

Isaiah's own sinfulness

" 'Woe to me!' I cried. 'I am ruined! For I am a man of unclean lips, and I live among a people of unclean lips, and my eyes have seen the King, the LORD Almighty' " (Isaiah 6:5).

You can always tell the people who haven't seen themselves in light of the holiness of God because they are the ones always pointing fingers of blame and looking at somebody else's sins—self-appointed vigilantes of righteousness who are so busy pointing out the speck in your eye that they overlook the railroad tie protruding from their own.

Isaiah had been pronouncing woes upon the sinners (Isaiah 5:8–30). Now, finding himself in the awesome presence of a holy God, he becomes profoundly aware of his own imperfections. This will happen to us, too, as we draw near to God. *You cannot experience true conversion until you first realize your own utter lostness and depravity without God.* "As long as we compare ourselves with other people, we can deceive ourselves that we are not that bad [an end-time delusion]. But when we compare ourselves to God, we see just how unrighteous we truly are."[3]

In the light of God's holiness, Isaiah's inner thoughts and motives are exposed. He stands naked and without excuse before God. He has been searched, and his anxious thoughts and wicked ways appear before him. He now sees himself utterly sinful, undone in God's presence. "My eyes have seen the King, the LORD Almighty," he cries. There's only one fate for him and for his people—annihilation.

But there's something else God wants His servant to see.

> No matter how bad things look here,
>
> . . . the truth is *the whole earth is full of God's glory.*

God's forgiveness

"Then one of the seraphim flew to me with a live coal in his hand, which he had taken with tongs from the altar. With it he touched my mouth and said, 'See, this has touched your lips; your guilt is taken away and your sin atoned for' " (Isaiah 6:6, 7).

At the depths of Isaiah's despair, he experienced the depths of God's grace. It's when we hit rock bottom that we discover God is still there! As Jonah discovered in the belly of a great fish, there's nowhere we can escape the goodness of God! Remember His glory fills the whole earth! *As holy as God is, His glory is most clearly seen in His mercy.*

> As holy as God is,
>
> His glory is most clearly
>
> seen in His mercy.

When God declared His name to Moses, He said, "The LORD, the LORD, the compassionate and gracious God, slow to anger, abounding in love and faithfulness, maintaining love to thousands, and forgiving wickedness, rebellion and sin" (Exodus 34:6, 7). And this is the glory of God—that God doesn't smite sinners; He saves them.

"Imagine the power of the moment," Craig Groeschel writes. "Isaiah has never been more aware of his guilt, his sin, his shame. And with one touch from God's being, his sin was gone. Forgotten. Forgiven. First, unconditional grace. Then, uncontainable gratitude."[4]

The call

> Then I heard the voice of the Lord saying, "Whom shall I send? And who will go for us?"
>
> And I said, "Here am I. Send me!" (Isaiah 6:8).

Once we see the holiness of God, our own sinfulness in light of that holiness, and we experience the forgiveness of God, then, out of uncontainable gratitude, we're shaped and ready to pray the powerful prayer, *Send me! Use me!*

Now think. Why would this awesome God, who directs the affairs of men, whose glory fills the whole earth, who sits on a sapphire throne encircled by an emerald rainbow, where lightning flashes and thunder peals, surrounded by millions of angelic beings whose voices of praise shake the foundations of the temple? Why would this God ask this question as if He needed help and His options were limited?

Why not send angels—the "burning ones"—who minister in His

immediate presence? It seems like a no-brainer, right? Wrong. Though they would do it faster and more efficiently, "Christ does not choose angels who have never fallen, but human beings, men of like passions with those they seek to save."[5]

As crazy as it seems (and it looks crazier all the time!), God uses forgiven human beings precisely because they have been forgiven. We know what it's like to be weak, what it's like to break our promises, what it's like to doubt, and what it's like to mess up and do stupid things. The angels don't. "Having been in peril themselves, they [humans] are acquainted with the dangers and difficulties of the way, and for this reason are called to reach out for others in like peril."[6] *We are searched, awakened, and broken to be sent to save.*

> *We are searched, awakened, and broken to be sent to save.*

God gives to you and me the privilege of being His first responders. He wants us to be like the firefighters and marines who, instead of running away from trouble, are the first ones to run toward it. The world is on fire, and it thinks its only hope comes from Washington, DC. But hope comes only from the One who sits on the throne. And that One is looking for some Isaiahs to get off the pew and into the game where the action is.

"Our heavenly Father has chosen to make Himself dependent *on people* to finish His conquest of sin," writes Douglas Cooper.

It will be the cooperation of human beings with divine beings that will defeat evil permanently. In a strange and ironic turnabout Satan is to be "bested" by the members of the very race he led astray! Nothing could demonstrate more effectively the superiority of love over selfishness, the power of compassion over coercion!

His honor, His very name and reputation in the universe rest in your hands and mind. *For this reason Christians are the most important people in the world right now!*[7]

"Who will go?"

The question still waits for an answer. Are Christians the most important people in the world right now? To whom? Each other? Based on our passion for talking among ourselves, I'd have to agree. We love to start new Bible studies and small groups for our own spiritual edification and enjoyment. And while there's nothing wrong with enjoying a good Bible study, the question God asked is not "Who will stay and study?" but "Who will *go?*"

In his book *The Missing Power*, Paulo Macena writes, "How sad is it to emphasize having another Bible study amongst ourselves on Saturday afternoons while never engaging in mission outside of the church's walls? . . . How relevant would a doctor be who completed ten specialized studies, displaying many different certificates on the wall, all while neglecting to treat anyone? Instead of saving lives, they continue to invite other doctors to meet with them to continue studying the benefits of treating the sick."[8]

Dr. Macena goes on to quote Oswald J. Smith, who says, " 'No one has the right to hear the gospel twice, while there remains someone who has not heard it once.' God called us not to study the great commission, but to share the great commission. We need to focus outside the church and stop having another Bible study to ourselves without intentionally bringing visitors to be part of it."[9]

Boldly go where only God has asked you to go

The opening narration of the *Star Trek* movies and TV episodes ends with the famous line, "To boldly go where no man has gone before!" *(Cue inspiring music!)* When we think about answering God's call to go for Him, we're often intimidated by the bigness of the enterprise. (See what I did there?) Maybe we need to stop trying to go where no man (or woman) has gone before and simply go where God directs us to go.

> We often fear the Lord will send us to some remote place in the mission field when the mission field He wants to send us to is the one in our own home.

Did God ask you to go door-to-door, give a Bible study, or preach a sermon? Maybe He did; maybe He didn't. But the one thing He has asked of all of us is to be witnesses for Him. *A witness is not something you do, but rather something you are.* Simply tell what happened to you. What have you seen? What have you experienced? God is on trial in the universe. He's accused of being unfair, uncaring, cruel, and severe. What light can you shed on the Accused? Please take the stand. State your name for the record. What has He done for you? "Can I get a witness?" God cries. "Please? Somebody? Anybody?"

We often fear the Lord will send us to some remote place in the mission field when the mission field He wants to send us to is the one in our own home. Start there. "Lord, send me first to my knees and then to my spouse to serve in love and humility. Send me first to my knees, then to that coworker or boss who pushes me to the edge of my Christianity to serve in love and humility. Send me first to my knees and then to that Black Lives Matter protester, that police officer, that conservative, that liberal, that Planned Parenthood worker, that pro-life advocate, that atheist, or that Christian nationalist to serve in love and humility."

"Who will go for us?" is the question that still awaits an answer in the closing moments of Earth's history. It's a closing question that can only be answered by those who have seen the holiness of God, their own sinfulness, and God's forgiveness and, in gratitude, are willing to go for Him.

Disturb me, Lord

Though written more than four hundred years ago, a prayer attributed to Sir Francis Drake, an English sea captain who lived from 1540 to 1596, is the right prayer for these closing hours of Earth's history. It's not an easy prayer to pray, but for those preparing to meet the Lord in peace, it's an absolute necessity.

> Disturb us, Lord, when we are too well pleased with ourselves, when our dreams have come true because we have dreamed too little, when we arrived safely because we sailed too close to the shore.
>
> Disturb us, Lord, when with the abundance of things we possess, we have lost our thirst for the waters of life; having fallen in love with life, we have ceased to dream of eternity, and in our efforts to build a new earth, we have allowed our vision of the new heaven to dim.
>
> Disturb us, Lord, to dare more boldly, to venture on wider seas, where storms will show your mastery; where losing sight of land, we shall find the stars. We ask you to push back the horizon of our hopes; and to push back the future in strength, courage, hope, and love.
>
> This we ask in the name of our Captain, who is Jesus Christ. Amen![10]

This kind of prayer reflects the primitive godliness we must have before Jesus comes again. And praying it is the only way you and I will ever be a danger to the kingdom of darkness. *To live and pray comfortably is to be a laughingstock to Satan's kingdom and a shame to God's.*

This is our time to get in the game and make a difference. Seek God and pray big. God is looking for someone to represent Him to this dying world. He's calling you! Will you say, Here I am, search me; here I am, wake me; here I am, break me; here I am, send me?

Closing Prayer

Send me, Lord, to bring light. Send me, Lord, to bring joy. Send me, Lord, to bring hope. But first, cleanse me of all of my foolishness and forgive my sins. Give me a new vision of who You are and who I am so that I may rightly represent You and prove Satan, not You, a liar.

My Closing Prayer

Write yours here: ____

____

____

____

____

---

1. Morris Venden, *Modern Parables* (Nampa, ID: Pacific Press®, 1998), 109, 110.

2. Craig Groeschel, *Dangerous Prayers* (Grand Rapids, MI: Zondervan, 2020), 109.

3. Groeschel, 128.

4. Groeschel, 129, 130.

5. Ellen G. White, *The Desire of Ages* (Mountain View, CA: Pacific Press®, 1940), 296.

6. White, 297.

7. Douglas Cooper, *Living in Our Finest Hour* (Mountain View, CA: Pacific Press®, 1982), 11; emphasis in the original.

8. Paulo Macena, *The Missing Power* (Silver Spring, MD: General Conference of Seventh-day Adventists Ministerial Association, 2017), 38.

9. Oswald J. Smith, quoted in Macena, 38.

10. Francis Drake, quoted in Groeschel, *Dangerous Prayers*, 157, 158.

BEFORE YOU CONTINUE

I pray you have been challenged by what you have read so far. If not, I have failed as a writer and as a preacher of the gospel. Why do we read books or listen to sermons, if not to grow and be stretched out of our comfort zones so that, ultimately, we "become mature, attaining to the whole measure of the fullness of Christ" (Ephesians 4:13)?

If you haven't been challenged yet, the following chapter may provide such a challenge. There's no denying how politically charged the atmosphere is at the present moment. It seems we have to be muzzled into insipid silence on almost any issue in the common discourse for fear of provoking an angry or polarized reaction. The mere mention of certain names or controversies can turn a person's heart to ice or lava, depending on where one stands politically. And, sad to say, this is true in the church as well.

Let me be clear. This is *not* a political book. It's a book about revival prayer in the last days—days that are charged politically, socially, religiously, and culturally with passions that are sometimes sublime and often ridiculous. We don't have to align ideologically with the things happening in our culture to learn from them. But learn from them, we must. The reader may find some of this next chapter's content to be provocative. I hope it is. Not because I have a hidden political agenda, but because I believe God has an overt spiritual agenda to push us out of our comfort zones and into a revolution of the Spirit that is "exceedingly abundantly above all that we ask or think" (Ephesians 3:20, NKJV).

Thomas Paine was right in saying, "These are the times that try men's souls." These are our times and our souls being tried. How then shall we pray? The "summer" intercessor and "sunshine" pray-er will not fare well in the times of winter ahead. Let us "be prepared in season and out of season" (2 Timothy 4:2) to be the answer to the prayers God is giving us to pray right now.

Part Two

REVIVAL UPRISINGS

No one calls on your name or strives to lay hold of you.
—Isaiah 64:7

Is that true of me, Lord? Do I not strive to lay hold of You like the unclean woman who touched the hem of Your garment? She knew what she wanted—healing—and where to get it: You. She would not let the crowd or protocol or the possible negative consequences stop her from laying hold of You. Her boldness was an act of faith that released healing virtue from You. Am I that bold? Am I striving as she did to seize hold of You?

Maybe I'm not as desperate. Maybe I can get along without Your healing power at work in my life. Maybe I don't see my lukewarmness as quite the curse that she saw her hemorrhage. But we're hemorrhaging, Lord. In many ways, we're bleeding internally and losing vitality in our preaching and in our ability to connect with a world that increasingly gets along without us.

Stop the bleeding, Lord. Help me to see my true need and to exercise the same bold faith that woman did to lay hold of You.

—Randy's journal, 10/7/19

6

"GOOD TROUBLE"

*Jesus entered the temple courts and drove out all who were
buying and selling there. He overturned the tables of the money
changers and the benches of those selling doves. "It is written," he
said to them, " 'My house will be called a house of prayer.' "*
—Matthew 21:12, 13

*Never, ever be afraid to make some noise
and get in good trouble, necessary trouble.*
—John Lewis, US congressman

We may not have chosen the time, but the time has chosen us." These words spoken by John Lewis, the late congressman and civil rights icon, reflect the zeitgeist of the hour.

We didn't choose the time, but for some reason, known only to God, He chose you and me to be here now. To do what? To be born again, as we saw earlier in this book. To rediscover the fundamental essence of what it means to be a Christian. To examine ourselves to see whether we are in the faith.

But God and the times may have chosen us for more. May I suggest that we're here to do something else that John Lewis said: to get in "good trouble."

"Never, ever be afraid to make some noise and get in good trouble," said Lewis, "necessary trouble." At this time of testing, when God is revealing what's in the hearts of His people, I'm under the conviction that we need to be troubled. Is it OK if the Spirit of God disturbs our peace? Here's some breaking news: *He's going to anyway, so buckle up!*

In September of 2018, sports apparel giant Nike stirred controversy with an ad campaign featuring the voice and face of National Football League quarterback Colin Kaepernick, who was known for kneeling during the

77

national anthem to bring attention to racial injustice. Superimposed over a close-up of Colin's face are these words: "Believe in something. Even if it means sacrificing everything."

The ad sparked immediate controversy and lit up the Twittersphere with calls for boycotts against Nike from some and praise from others. I remember seeing videos of people burning their Nike-branded athletic gear in protest over the company's partnership with someone perceived to be anti-American. However you may feel about Nike or Kaepernick, one thing is clear: both parties were willing to depart from the status quo—to make some "good trouble."

Revivals generally get started when the status quo becomes unbearable.

All this got me thinking about revival. We talk about it a lot at prayer meetings and retreats. But what do revival and good trouble have in common? *Revivals generally get started when the status quo becomes unbearable.* I've heard it described as "the crystallization of discontent." It's when the pain of staying the same becomes greater than the pain of change, and inaction is intolerable.

Revival uprisings

What do we mean by *revival*? Colin Whittaker defines it as "those special seasons of divine visitation when God the Holy Ghost quickens and stirs the slumbering Church of God. Believers are set ablaze for Christ and the power of God is so manifest in prevailing prayer and anointed preaching of the gospel that the most hardened and skeptical unbelievers are brought under great conviction of sin, leading in turn to genuine repentance and saving faith in the Lord Jesus Christ, through His death on the cross and resurrection."[1]

Revival is what happens when the Holy Spirit is in control of the church and is unleashed in society. And the hunger to experience Jesus in His fullness causes the saints of God to refuse the empty calories of business as usual.

In *Revivals: Their Laws and Leaders*, James Burns writes, "Preceding Revivals there often seems to be 'a widespread spirit of dissatisfaction among those God is preparing for what He is about to do. The heart of man begins to cry out for God, for spiritual certainties, for fresh visions. From a faint desire this multiplies as it widens, until it becomes a vast human need; until in its urgency it seems to beat with violence at the very gates of heaven."[2]

Sound aggressive? It is. This is a revival uprising born from discontent. The "spirit of dissatisfaction" produces meaningful spiritual actions that move mountains of generational and institutional death. These revival uprisings are the spiritual counterpart to the many social uprisings we've witnessed around the globe in response to social injustice.

Describing the "agapic" support of student activists by some University of Missouri faculty and staff, Stephanie Shonekan, chair of the Department of Black Studies, wrote, "Nobody asked us to do it. Something moved deep in our spirits, moved us from sympathy to empathy to action."[3] That "something" was the crystallization of discontent and costly agape love.

"Sympathy is nice," Shonekan explains. "Empathy is nicer. But they are both inadequate for real change. . . . Bottom line, expending sympathy or empathy costs us very little. We do the 'good deed,' we pat ourselves on the back, and we return to our normal lives. The 'good deed' rarely changes anything substantial."[4]

Substantial change requires substantial action—action that often disturbs our peace and causes trouble, good trouble. Consider with me some good troublemakers from Scripture.

Bartimaeus

Then they came to Jericho. As Jesus and his disciples, together with a large crowd, were leaving the city, a blind man, Bartimaeus (which means "son of Timaeus"), was sitting by the roadside begging. When he heard that it was Jesus of Nazareth, he began to shout, "Jesus, Son of David, have mercy on me!"

Many rebuked him and told him to be quiet, but he shouted all the more, "Son of David, have mercy on me!"

Jesus stopped and said, "Call him."

So they called to the blind man, "Cheer up! On your feet! He's calling you." Throwing his cloak aside, he jumped to his feet and came to Jesus.

"What do you want me to do for you?" Jesus asked him.

The blind man said, "Rabbi, I want to see" (Mark 10:46–51).

Bartimaeus was not to be denied. With his shouts, he was beating "with violence at the very gates of heaven." He knew who Jesus was and the opportunity that His presence provided. Do we?

" 'Go,' said Jesus, 'your faith has healed you' " (verse 52). What faith? Bartimaeus's faith to make some noise and call on Jesus. That's good trouble.

The woman with the hemorrhage

And a woman was there who had been subject to bleeding for twelve years. She had suffered a great deal under the care of many doctors and had spent all she had, yet instead of getting better she grew worse. When she heard about Jesus, she came up behind him in the crowd and touched his cloak, because she thought, "If I just touch his clothes, I will be healed." Immediately her bleeding stopped and she felt in her body that she was freed from her suffering.

At once Jesus realized that power had gone out from him. He turned around in the crowd and asked, "Who touched my clothes?"

"You see the people crowding against you," his disciples answered, "and yet you can ask, 'Who touched me?' "

But Jesus kept looking around to see who had done it. Then the woman, knowing what had happened to her, came and fell at his feet and, trembling with fear, told him the whole truth. He said to her, "Daughter, your faith has healed you. Go in peace and be freed from your suffering" (Mark 5:25–34).

Again, what faith? The woman's faith to break protocol, disrupt the procession, and touch Jesus. In that time and culture, a woman didn't touch a man in public who was not her husband. And under no circumstances was an *unclean* woman to touch a holy man, thereby defiling him. She could have faced severe punishment or death for doing what she did. But her desperation drove her to endure some necessary trouble.

Ceiling crashers

How about the four friends who tore a hole in a roof to get their paralyzed friend to Jesus (Mark 2:1–12)? As Jesus brushed away the debris and squinted His eyes to adjust to the sunlight streaming down on Him from the ceiling that was now destroyed, is that irritation or delight on His face in response to such boldness?

"When Jesus saw their faith, he said to the paralyzed man, 'Son, your sins are forgiven' " (verse 5). Whose faith? The friends' faith to disrupt the service and break open the roof to get their friend to Jesus.

Temple uprising

Not to be outdone, Jesus knew when and where to make some good trouble of His own—necessary trouble. Jesus was initiating the greatest revival and reformation of all time. He was not another prophet, not another teacher, not another scripture, but the Living Word. And in the middle of God's "new thing" (Isaiah 43:19), the people who claimed to be God's were clinging to the same old thing. And it became unbearable.

"When it was almost time for the Jewish Passover, Jesus went up to Jerusalem. In the temple courts he found people selling cattle, sheep and doves, and others sitting at tables exchanging money. So he made a whip out of cords, and drove all from the temple courts, both sheep and cattle; he scattered the coins of the money changers and overturned their tables. To those who sold doves he said, 'Get these out of here! Stop turning my Father's house into a market!' " (John 2:13–16).

And His protest was about prayer! In each of the synoptic Gospel accounts of this incident, Jesus states the motive for His "madness": "My house will be called a house of prayer, but you are making it a 'den of robbers' " (Matthew 21:13; see also Mark 11:17; Luke 19:46). Sometimes effectual fervent prayer calls for us to disturb our peace, shake things up, flip some of our ideological tables, and "beat with violence at the very gates of heaven."

He speaks, and His clear, ringing voice—the same that upon Mount Sinai proclaimed the law that priests and rulers are transgressing—is heard echoing through the arches of the temple: "Take these things hence; make not My Father's house an house of merchandise."

Slowly descending the steps, and raising the scourge of cords gathered up on entering the enclosure, He bids the bargaining company depart from the precincts of the temple. With a zeal and severity He has never before manifested, He overthrows the tables of the money-changers. The coin falls, ringing sharply upon the marble pavement. None presume to question His authority. None dare stop to gather up their ill-gotten gain. Jesus does not smite them with the whip of cords, but in His hand that simple scourge seems terrible as a flaming sword. Officers of the temple, speculating priests, brokers and cattle traders, with their sheep and oxen, rush from the place, with the one thought of escaping from the condemnation of His presence.

A panic sweeps over the multitude, who feel the overshadowing of His divinity. Cries of terror escape from hundreds of blanched lips. Even the disciples tremble. They are awestruck by the words and manner of Jesus, so unlike His usual demeanor. They remember that it is written of Him, "The zeal of Thine house hath eaten Me up." Psalm 69:9. Soon the tumultuous throng with their merchandise are far removed from the temple of the Lord. The courts are free from unholy traffic, and a deep silence and solemnity settles upon the scene of confusion. The presence of the Lord, that of old sanctified the mount, has now made sacred the temple reared in His honor.[5]

Jesus created a disturbance to clear space for prayer. What are we willing to disturb to make room for God? Prayer had been hijacked by profit. Communion was traded for cash. Intercession came with interest. And Jesus wasn't having it. Revival was required first at the house of God, and it took some good trouble to get it started.

Let me ask you this: When are we going to stop preaching about revival and start disturbing the peace of our programs to seek it? There comes a point when talk must be followed by action. The world advocating for social change gets it. The church advocating for spiritual change often doesn't.

Before the pandemic, Suzette and I joined a local gym. Our metabolisms, which had been rocket fast in our younger years, were turtle slow in our middle years. Our weight had plateaued. Our bodies had adjusted to what we were doing, but we kept doing it, hoping for different results. Finally, we realized we had to do something different. We had to disturb the peace of our plateau. And that goes for the spiritual plateau too. At some point, wishful thinking must become an unrelenting demand.

According to your demand

"Only to those who wait humbly upon God, who watch for His guidance and grace, is the Spirit given. The power of God awaits their demand and reception."[6]

How do you understand *demand*? It could be like Jacob wrestling with the Lord, saying, "I will not let you go unless you bless me" (Genesis 32:26). Or it can be "the state of being wanted or sought for purchase or use."[7]

At camp meetings, Wi-Fi is always in high demand. People come into guest services, and often the first thing they ask is, "What is the Wi-Fi password?" The Wi-Fi signal is spotty at the campgrounds, and there are times when everyone wants internet access at the same time. Those are times of peak demand. We want it. Expect it. Even demand it. *(Heaven forbid we aren't able to access our email or post to Facebook during a spiritual retreat!)* Demand for Wi-Fi is high.

There are other times (usually in the middle of the night) when the demand is low. Unlike a camp meeting's Wi-Fi, the power of God has unlimited bandwidth, and it is there for the asking. But is demand high or low among us? We say we want power but settle for programs. We claim to want revival but settle for ritual. We keep doing the same things, expecting different results.

God wants to disturb the peace of our resistance to having our peace disturbed. It's been said that nothing ruins a cemetery like a good resurrection. It messes up the whole concept. But some people would rather not be disturbed from their pew coffins. Instead of "Lazarus, come forth," they would prefer to hear, "Lazarus, turn over!"

But others desperately want to awaken from slumber. "Then [with a deep longing] you will seek Me and require Me [as a vital necessity] and [you will] find Me when you search for Me with all your heart" (Jeremiah 29:13, AMP). Your demand will bring healing.

Are our prayers a disturbance?

At camp meeting a couple of years ago (real, not virtual), I was the early morning devotional speaker. I remember asking the crowd whether they thought it mattered to the city of Auburn that we were gathered there for ten days every June. Did anyone in town know or care that we were there? There are other annual events that occur in the greater Seattle area that everyone knows about. You know when Comic Con comes to town, when it's PrideFest, when it's Seafair, and so on. We even know when the vegetarians come to Seattle for Vegfest! But does anyone know when the Adventists gather for their annual spiritual convocation?

I pressed with a better question: "Does it matter in hell that we're here? Do the demons care that we're here? Are our prayers a disturbance to the kingdom of darkness?" I've heard it said that we should live our lives in such a way that when we arise in the morning, the devil says, "Oh no, they're awake!" To that, I would add, "And they're going to make trouble!"

God wants to disturb the peace of our resistance to having our peace disturbed.

"There is nothing that Satan fears so much as that the people of God shall clear the way by removing every hindrance, so that the Lord can pour out His Spirit upon a languishing church and an impenitent congregation."[8]

To *languish* means to be "weak or feeble; droop; fade. To lose vigor and vitality [impotent]. To undergo neglect or experience prolonged inactivity. . . . To be subjected to delay or disregard; be ignored [like Bartimaeus, the woman with the hemorrhage, and the paralytic]. To pine with desire or longing."[9]

Impenitent means "not feeling regret for one's sin or sins."[10] In other words, you're in bad shape but are OK with it. Unlike Bartimaeus and the others who disturbed the peace, the church has made peace with its paralysis. Prolonged inactivity has become the status quo. There's nothing that Jesus wants more than for His people to disturb the status quo—to cause necessary trouble for the enemy's kingdom.

In his book *Letters to the Church*, Francis Chan writes about the time he and his daughter visited an underground church gathering in China some years ago. He recalls hearing the young people praying so passionately, begging God to send them to some of the most dangerous places. They were actually hoping to die as martyrs.

Francis writes,

> I had never seen anything like it. I still can't get over the fearless passion for Jesus this church embodied. As they shared stories of persecution I sat in amazement and asked for more stories. After a while they asked why I was so intrigued. I told them that the church in America was nothing like this. I can't tell you how embarrassing it was to try to explain to them that people attend 90-minute services once a week in buildings and that's what we call church. I told them about how people switch churches if they find better teaching, more exciting music, or most robust programs for their children. As I began to describe the church in America, they began to laugh. Not just small chuckles, they were laughing hysterically. I felt like a stand-up comedian, but I was simply describing the American church as I've experienced it. They found it laughable that we could read the same scriptures they were reading and then create something so incongruent.[11]

And Satan laughs too. As long as the church remains in this condition, he has nothing to worry about.

But "when the way is prepared for the Spirit of God, the blessing will come. Satan can no more hinder a shower of blessing from descending upon God's people than he can close the windows of heaven that rain cannot come upon the earth. Wicked men and devils cannot hinder the work of God, or shut out His presence from the assemblies of His people, if they will, with subdued, contrite hearts, confess and put away their sins, and in faith claim His promises."[12] *Revival comes only in answer to prayer—prayer that disturbs the peace of paralysis.*

Heaven's divine interruption

The phrase "we interrupt this broadcast" has been used frequently by radio and TV networks when breaking into a program in progress to deliver important news or information. The descent of the Spirit at Pentecost was Heaven's divine interruption of the spiritual status quo in progress and the key to victory in the real war of the worlds, known as the great controversy. Oh, how we need a repeat of that disturbance today! In these last days, and in preparation for the final crisis, *God wants to interrupt your regularly scheduled life with His Holy Spirit, so you begin to really live.*

Before Jesus ascended to heaven, He told His disciples that some good trouble from heaven was coming. "I am going to send you what my Father has promised; but stay in the city until you have been clothed with power from on high" (Luke 24:49). From "on high," not from online. The power is from God, not from Google; it is of Heaven, not of Earth.

> *God wants to interrupt your regularly scheduled life with His Holy Spirit, so you begin to really live.*

What if the disciples did not wait to be clothed with power from on high? Where would that leave them? *Unclothed, in weakness from below!* And how many of us start our days exactly like that! All dressed up and spiritually naked! Looking good but without any power to love other people; no power to honor my spouse; no power to properly guide and nurture my children; no power to reflect Jesus in my workplace; no power to do anything but be my weak, unregenerate self.

And the church body is no better off. With all our programs, committees, and policies, if we don't wait to be clothed with power from on high, we are unclothed, in weakness from below! The scandal is that everyone can see that the "emperor" has no clothes! We must have the baptism of the Holy Spirit, or we die! We will not be able to give any "convincing proofs" to each other or the world that Jesus is alive (Acts 1:3)!

How should we wait for Heaven's divine interruption? Like the disciples did.

> As the disciples waited for the fulfillment of the promise, they humbled their hearts in true repentance and confessed their unbelief. . . .
>
> The disciples prayed with intense earnestness for a fitness to meet men and in their daily intercourse to speak words that would lead sinners to Christ. Putting away all differences, all desire for the

supremacy, they came close together in Christian fellowship. . . .

These days of preparation were days of deep heart searching. The disciples felt their spiritual need and cried to the Lord for the holy unction that was to fit them for the work of soul saving. They did not ask for a blessing for themselves merely. They were weighted with the burden of the salvation of souls. They realized that the gospel was to be carried to the world, and they claimed the power that Christ had promised.[13]

Please don't rush through that passage. I want to interrupt your regularly paced reading of this chapter to focus on this special message. Go back, and you'll see several keys to Heaven-interrupted praying:

- "Humbled their hearts in true repentance."
- "Confessed their unbelief."
- "Intense earnestness for a fitness to . . . lead sinners to Christ."
- "Putting away all differences."
- "Putting away . . . all desire for the supremacy."
- "Christian fellowship." (That's accountability.)
- "Deep heart searching."
- "Felt their spiritual need."
- "Cried to the Lord for the holy unction."
- "Weighted with the burden of the salvation of souls."
- "Claimed the power that Christ promised."

My friends, *heavenly interruptions are preceded by earthly intercessions.* This kind of praying taps into God's agenda instead of ours. And the failure to pray this way is why so many Christians live less than abundant lives personally and struggle with a lack of power in their relationships. Because when the Week of Prayer is over, when the special spiritual retreat ends, when the sun sets on Sabbath—as the old TV and radio announcers used to say, "We now return you to your regularly scheduled program already in progress"—we resume right where we left off! I know because I resume! I resume. And resuming will be the death of us!

If all we do after COVID is return to our regularly scheduled programming, we will miss out on Pentecost! We cannot *resume*; we must *repent.*

In the last year, we cannot say that "the things of earth" have grown "strangely dim."[14] Rather, they have grown strangely strong and, for many, have dimmed the light of God's glory and grace. The virus has been all too real. The fear, the anger, the denial, the election, the protests, the conspiracy theories, the Capitol siege, the vaccines, the hate crimes—they're all too real, and in contrast, the Spirit seems like a dream. And that means we've got to ditch our old programming and take up Heaven's programming: a call to prayer that will require time, humility, faith, honesty, death to self, accountability, spiritual hunger, and looking outside of ourselves to the needs of others.

The disciples were in the right place at the right time doing the right thing for the right reasons, and it was then that God broke in with a special bulletin: "We interrupt the regularly scheduled program to bring you this special heavenly presentation!"

Pentecost was the interruption of the regular programming of Pharisaical teaching; the regular programming of sectarian, prejudicial, nationalistic thinking; the regular programming of relational strife, jealousy, racial bigotry, and gender supremacy. *The Holy Spirit was Heaven's special presentation of Jesus, who returned to Earth in wind and fire to breathe life into the dead and to burn up the grave clothes.* He came to empower the church to make some good trouble!

Challenge

So what are we going to do? I challenge you to disturb the peace and to pray Habakkuk's prayer:

> LORD, I have heard of your fame;
> > I stand in awe of your deeds, LORD.
> Repeat them in our day,
> > in our time make them known (Habakkuk 3:2).

This will surely cause a disturbance to you, your church, your home, and more. Will you do it?

> You who call on the LORD,
> > give yourselves no rest,
> and give him no rest till he establishes Jerusalem
> > and makes her the praise of the earth (Isaiah 62:6, 7).

I challenge you to believe in something and to pray about the right things, even if that means sacrificing everything. That's the only way things change. That's the only way revival comes. Isn't it high time to flip some tables on the enemy? Are you up for some good trouble?

Closing Prayer

Lord, I need You to interrupt my regular "programming" and prayers with something from Heaven. Make me as nauseated as You are with normal, insipid, and Spirit-starved Christianity. Stir me to good trouble. Jesus, make me a praise to heaven and a threat to hell, and do the same in Your church. We need more than sympathy and sermons. We need actions—the actions of a people who are willing to have their peace disturbed and, on their knees, "beat with violence at the very gates of heaven." Jesus, Son of David, have mercy on us! Have mercy on me.

My Closing Prayer

Write yours here: ____

____

____

____

____

____

1. Colin Whittaker, *Great Revivals* (London: William Collins, Sons, 1990), 21.

2. James Burns, *Revivals: Their Laws and Leaders* (Grand Rapids, MI: Baker Book House, 1960), quoted in Whittaker, *Great Revivals*, 68.

3. Stephanie Shonekan, " 'We People Who Are Darker Than Blue,' " in *Campus Uprisings: How Student Activists and Collegiate Leaders Resist Racism and Create Hope*, ed. Ty-Ron M. O. Douglas, Kmt G. Shockley, and Ivory Toldson (New York: Teachers College Press, 2020), 10.

4. Shonekan, 9.

5. Ellen G. White, *The Desire of Ages* (Mountain View, CA: Pacific Press®, 1940), 158.

6. White, 672.

7. Dictionary.com, s.v. "demand," accessed August 6, 2020, https://www.dictionary.com/browse/demand.

8. Ellen G. White, *Selected Messages*, bk. 1 (Washington, DC: Review and Herald®, 1958), 124.

9. Dictionary.com, s.v. "languish," accessed August 6, 2020, https://www.dictionary.com/browse/languish.

10. Dictionary.com, s.v. "impenitent," accessed August 6, 2020, https://www.dictionary.com/browse/impenitent.

11. Francis Chan, *Letters to the Church* (Colorado Springs, CO: David C. Cook, 2018), 154, 155.

12. White, *Selected Messages*, 1:124.

13. Ellen G. White, *The Acts of the Apostles* (Mountain View, CA: Pacific Press®, 1911), 36, 37.

14. Helen Howarth Lemmel, "Turn Your Eyes Upon Jesus," in *The Seventh-day Adventist Hymnal* (Hagerstown, MD: Review and Herald®, 1985), no. 290.

7

GET USED TO DIFFERENT

*"I have much more to say to you,
more than you can now bear.
But when he, the Spirit of truth, comes,
he will guide you into all the truth."*
—John 16:12, 13

*Let me tell you that the Lord will work in this last work in
a manner very much out of the common order of things, and
in a way that will be contrary to any human planning.*
—Ellen G. White

My new favorite TV program is *The Chosen* series—the first multiseason show about the life of Christ. What I love about it is the realistic presentation of the personalities of the men and women Jesus chose to follow Him. They are not stained-glass saints by any stretch of the imagination. The characters are given backstories that help the audience connect with them on an emotional level.

I have *The Chosen* app on my phone, and as I'm writing this, I'm watching a replay of the season two premiere that was livestreamed a couple of days ago. More than eighty-two thousand were watching on YouTube, fifty thousand were watching on the app, and there were no numbers available from Facebook. Excitement is running high. I can't wait to see how the story progresses in the first episode of the new season.

But the signature moment, for me, from the first season is the calling of Levi Matthew. The writers did a good job of making Matthew extremely unlikable. Matthew's character is hated by everyone. As a tax collector for the despised Romans, his own family is ashamed of him. He's OCD, an outcast, and seems to have only two emotions—extreme anger or extreme sadness. And he doesn't know how to process either one. He's isolated and alone.

Then one day, Jesus passes by Matthew's tax booth, calls him by name, and says, "Follow Me."

"Me?" Matthew replies incredulously.

"Yes, you," Jesus says.

Peter objects. "What are You doing? Do You have any idea what this guy has done? Do You even know him?"

Keeping His eyes fixed on Matthew, Jesus says, "Yes."

Instantly, Matthew leaves the booth.

"I don't get it," Peter says.

"You didn't get it when I chose you either," Jesus replies.

"But this is different," Peter retorts. "I'm not a tax collector."

Then Jesus utters my favorite line of season one: "Get used to different."

Jesus was different

Though those words aren't recorded in Scripture, Jesus said and did plenty of things that were different.

- When the Word became flesh and occupied the womb of an unwed Galilean teenager, only to be born in a cave with animals—*that was different.*
- When, at the age of twelve, He was found in the temple, amazing the teachers of the law in regard to the prophecies and giving them a depth of meaning that these expert theologians had not conceived of—*that was different.*
- When Jesus appeared on the banks of the Jordan to be baptized, "and as he was praying, heaven was opened and the Holy Spirit descended on him in bodily form like a dove. And a voice came from heaven: 'You are my Son, whom I love; with you I am well pleased' " (Luke 3:21, 22)—*that was different.*
- When Jesus told Simon to let down his nets for a catch in broad daylight, and after doing so against his will, so many fish swam into the nets that two boats were about to sink—*that was different.*
- When the woman caught in adultery was about to be stoned and, after challenging her accusers, Jesus told her He didn't condemn her and said, "Go now and leave your life of sin" (John 8:11)—*that was different.*
- When Jesus spoke to a storm and hushed it into silence—*that was different.*
- When He fed a multitude with a little boy's sack lunch and had leftovers to spare—*that was different.*

- When Jesus made a whip of cords and overturned the tables of the money changers who were turning His Father's house of prayer into a den of robbers—*that was different.*
- When Jesus raised a man to life who had been four days dead—*that was different!*
- When Jesus received and praised the devotion of a sinful woman who anointed His head and feet with expensive perfume and wiped His feet with her hair—*that was different.*
- When Jesus was mere hours away from the cross, and as a last act of love, He washed the feet of His self-seeking disciples, including the feet of His betrayer—*that was different.*
- When Jesus hung on the cross and prayed, "Father, forgive them, for they do not know what they are doing" (Luke 23:34)—*that was different!*
- And just before He ascended to heaven, when the disciples were again asking whether this was the time Israel was to be restored to prominence, Jesus said, "It is not for you to know the times or dates the Father has set by his own authority. But you will receive power when the Holy Spirit comes on you; and you will be my witnesses in Jerusalem, and in all Judea and Samaria, and to the ends of the earth" (Acts. 1:8). In other words, *get ready for different!*

And that's why it is such a tragedy for Christians to have such low expectations, to always play it safe, and to keep repeating things the way we've always done them. Our Savior, the Rabbi we follow, is all about different. He does things that we could never imagine. He is "the God who gives life to the dead and calls into being things that were not" (Romans 4:17).

Didn't see it coming

Who would have imagined that things could actually get better for the disciples with Jesus gone rather than there with them? It doesn't get any better than having Jesus in the flesh to walk and talk with, right? But Jesus had a surprise for His disciples.

They were praying, and "when the day of Pentecost came, they were all together in one place. Suddenly a sound like the blowing of a violent wind came from heaven and filled the whole house where they were sitting. They saw what seemed to be tongues of fire that separated and came to rest on each of them. All of them were filled with the Holy Spirit and began to speak in other tongues as the Spirit enabled them" (Acts 2:1–4).

No one saw that coming! God's presence was no longer on a mountain, in a cloud, or in the Most Holy Place of the temple. The glory of God, through the Holy Spirit, dwelt inside those men and women who were now empowered to change the world. *That was different!* And it wasn't long before that difference was clearly seen.

Stop being lame

Acts 4 finds Peter and John arrested and hauled before the Sanhedrin and threatened with punishment for healing in Jesus' name. In Acts 3, we read that Peter and John had surprised a crippled beggar in front of the gate called Beautiful as they were entering the temple to pray. According to Acts 3:2, the man was "lame from birth." His lameness was a congenital problem centered in his feet. The Greek word that Dr. Luke uses here implies that the paralysis was in the base or heels of his feet, in the socket of the ankle. The bones were out of place from birth. He had never walked, never known strength in his lower extremities, never ran, jumped, climbed, or swam.

Why is this important? Because it's not our first birth that matters, only the second. We're all born spiritual cripples (Psalm 51:5). None of us has ever walked uprightly (Romans 3:10–18). We're all born "*that* way." That's why we must be born again. This story proves that *when genetics meets Jesus, Jesus wins!* Even when a church is suffering from a dislocated spirit and is out of joint with Heaven, the Spirit of God can put it back together again!

Peter demands focus from the beggar. "Look at us!" (Acts 3:4). This is different. Nobody talks to the poor wretch as he begs. People merely give, or they ignore, but rare indeed is any conversation or eye contact. The man waits in full expectation of a large gift. He just has no idea how large. It's about to get different really quickly.

When genetics meets Jesus, Jesus wins!

"Then Peter said, 'Silver or gold I do not have' " (verse 6). How the man's face must have fallen! Did Peter demand his attention just to mock him? "But what I do have I give you. In the *name* of Jesus Christ of Nazareth, walk" (verse 6; emphasis added). Now *that was different!* That's not what the crippled man expected that day. He expected a few coins so he could continue his life of lameness. What he didn't expect was healing! He didn't expect transformation. He didn't expect a whole new life. But it was time for the lame man to get used to different!

Peter didn't have silver or gold, but what he had was infinitely greater. He gave the man the *name* of Jesus. And what a difference a name makes! Peter stood before the lame man representing the character of *Jehovah Ropheka*—"the God who heals." He stood before the beggar holding the master key to the treasury of Heaven. He stood before him in possession of kingdom authority to break the power of every demon in hell. Peter stood there in covenantal oneness with the Father, knowing that the name of Jesus is the badge of their relationship. Peter was protected by that name, and no weapon formed against him could prosper. He knew that all power had been given to His friend Jesus and because the Comforter had come and he had been baptized in the Holy Spirit, all that belonged to Jesus now belonged to him. He stood there bearing the reputation of Christ and His kingdom of love.

> *After an encounter with the name of Jesus, it was no longer acceptable to live in lameness!*

No wonder Peter could say, "Get up and walk!" Actually, it was a command to stop being lame. Listen to me! *After an encounter with the name of Jesus, it was no longer acceptable to live in lameness!* My friends, if the Resurrected One is dwelling in you by the Holy Spirit, *stop being lame*!

And that goes for the church too. Lameness and lukewarmness are the same things. In the closing hours of Earth's history, and in preparation for the final crisis, Jesus is saying to us, "Look at Me! Quit looking around at everything else going on, and focus on Me! Stop your lame gossip. Stop your lame petty infighting. Stop your lame works righteousness. Stop your lame excuses for holding onto un-Christlike attitudes and actions. Stop being lame; *rise and walk*!" What Jesus did through Peter and John for the lame man, He wants to do again for the church through the Holy Spirit.

It is for this miracle that Peter and John faced reprisals in Acts 4. While everyone else may have been rejoicing, the priests and members of the Sanhedrin were not. "They were greatly disturbed because the apostles were teaching the people, proclaiming in Jesus the resurrection of the dead. They seized Peter and John and, because it was evening, they put them in jail until the next day" (Acts 4:2, 3).

Don't miss this: *different faith often upsets those who don't have any.* The enemy gets mad when his captives go free. And when we wake up to different, he's ticked off. He wants to keep you and me sound asleep in our caskets of life—stress, denial, and depression.

Peter and John were no longer fishing. They were no longer vying for the seats of power in Christ's kingdom. They were no longer denying Christ with curses, cutting off people's ears, or praying for fire to come down and destroy those who were different from themselves. They were wide awake in the power of the Holy Spirit, living resurrected lives. And for those who've experienced what a difference resurrection makes, normal is a thing of the past.

Get used to taking Jesus seriously

The next day Peter and John were brought before the religious elite to explain their actions on behalf of the once-lame man. "By what power or what name did you do this?" they asked (verse 7).

> Then Peter, filled with the Holy Spirit, said to them: "Rulers and elders of the people! If we are being called to account today for an act of kindness shown to a man who was lame and are being asked how he was healed, then know this, you and all the people of Israel: It is by the name of Jesus Christ of Nazareth, whom you crucified but whom God raised from the dead, that this man stands before you healed. Jesus is
>
> " 'the stone you builders rejected,
> which has become the cornerstone.'
>
> "Salvation is found in no one else, for there is no other name under heaven given to mankind by which we must be saved."
> When they saw the courage of Peter and John and realized that they were unschooled, ordinary men, they were astonished and they took note that these men had been with Jesus (verses 8–13).

They were "astonished"! Why? Because *this was different*! These were "unschooled, ordinary men" speaking in the name of Jesus with power and boldness. They must have thought to themselves, *We've seen this before! This is Jesus all over again—Jesus 2.0! We thought we got rid of Him, but He's still here in these men!*

My friend, that's what the world should be saying about us: Jesus is still here through the church because we walk like Him, talk like Him, love like Him, and live like Him! I cringe to think how often the behavior of many "Christians" gives more evidence to the existence of Satan than to Christ!

Not so with Peter and John. Please note that these men were being punished for their audacity to take Jesus seriously. They took Jesus so seriously that they actually believed He could change the worst circumstances of the most broken people. Do we have that kind of audacity? Do I? Do we have the nerve to actually believe that God can change the worst circumstances of the most broken people? We better, or why waste the time? There are other things we could be doing. If you don't believe Jesus makes a difference and can change lives, I question your sanity for being here.

People who are getting used to different take Jesus seriously. This one factor sets the tone for the entire book of Acts. These are people who take Jesus seriously. It's not a game to them. It's not culture or habit or duty or form. It's eternal life to them, and nothing matters more. Would to God we would take Jesus seriously too. All the studies suggest that we do not. But you don't need a study to tell you that.

When do you take God seriously? Isn't it usually in a crisis? When do you take your health seriously? Isn't it usually when you're ill or waiting for a diagnosis?

Somewhere between this chapter and the previous one, I passed a kidney stone. It was my second one, but there was about a year and a half interval between them. I knew a second stone was still in my left kidney, but the doctor said it was a small one, and he'd keep an eye on it. In the meantime, I needed to drink more water, watch my fatty-food intake, blah, blah. The first stone was memorable, but as time passed, I went on with my life as usual. Until . . . You've heard of waiting for the other shoe to drop? Well, it wasn't a shoe, but it sure felt like one! When that pain hit, I got serious in a hurry. The crisis had come, and as I was getting a CT scan and fluids, I was all business. But ordinarily, we're just ordinary.

The same can be said of us spiritually. The sad thing is that you can be spiritually mediocre in this church and country—spiritually flabby—and still be average. And if the truth be known, being average, normal, and spiritually flabby is pretty OK by most Christians' standards. But most Christians are not our standard. Christ is the standard. When things seem just fine, we are unwilling to make the huge changes needed to get huge results. But in a time of drought, we don't need ordinary; we need to get used to different.

It's like the motivational poster showing a goldfish leaping from a bowl full of other goldfish into another bowl. The caption reads, "If you want something in your life you've never had, you'll have to do something you've never done." That something is following Jesus. That something is being different.

Get used to praying different

The council couldn't figure out what to do with these men because the miracle couldn't be denied. So they opted for containment to stop this "thing" from spreading (Acts 4:17). What thing? Could it be what God spoke through Isaiah when He said, "Forget the former things; do not dwell on the past. See, I am doing a new thing!" (Isaiah 43:18, 19)? Jesus was the "New Thing," the "Unprecedented Thing" (never known or done before), and so were His methods. Everything in the Old Testament had been leading up to Calvary and the big bang of Pentecost that followed. Before, God's glory was confined to the Most Holy Place in the temple; now, the Word of God was incarnate again in those who were boldly proclaiming it. The New Thing was Heaven invading Earth, and Jesus doing His thing through His newly resurrected body—the church!

One Jesus to deal with was bad enough, but now, in these men and their converts, Jesus was multiplied many times over! To keep *that* new thing from spreading, "they called them in again and commanded them not to speak or teach at all in the name of Jesus" (Acts 4:18). But if the Sanhedrin couldn't keep Jesus' dead body in the tomb, how in the world did they think they could keep His risen body and living Spirit contained? They couldn't.

"But Peter and John replied, 'Which is right in God's eyes: to listen to you, or to him? You be the judges! As for us, we cannot help speaking about what we have seen and heard' " (verses 19, 20).

Humiliated and befuddled by Peter and John's boldness and all the people praising God, the members of the Sanhedrin (the religious version of the Keystone Cops) threatened them and let them go.

Peter and John then went back to the church and told what had happened. Did they say, "We've got to take it easy on testifying and healing because the world is getting angry with us. We can still worship Jesus, but we've got to think about what it will mean if we keep on upsetting the powers that be. Maybe our faith is a little too dynamic, bold, and rowdy"? No! Rather than retreat into fear, they prayed!

"Sovereign Lord," they said, "you made the heavens and the earth and the sea, and everything in them. You spoke by the Holy Spirit through the mouth of your servant, our father David:

" 'Why do the nations rage
    and the peoples plot in vain?
The kings of the earth rise up

and the rulers band together
against the Lord
and against his anointed one.'

"Indeed Herod and Pontius Pilate met together with the Gentiles and the people of Israel in this city to conspire against your holy servant Jesus, whom you anointed. They did what your power and will had decided beforehand should happen. Now, Lord, consider their threats and enable your servants to speak your word with great boldness. Stretch out your hand to heal and perform signs and wonders through the name of your holy servant Jesus."

After they prayed, the place where they were meeting was shaken. And they were all filled with the Holy Spirit and spoke the word of God boldly (verses 24–31).

When you take Jesus seriously, you take prayer seriously. And when you take prayer seriously, that's when God takes your prayers seriously. Did you catch that last verse? "After they prayed, the place where they were meeting was shaken. And they were all filled with the Holy Spirit and spoke the word of God boldly." What a prayer meeting! Prayer that made the earth shake. *That was different!* And God is calling us to be different and pray some earthshaking prayers today.

> **When you take Jesus seriously, you take prayer seriously. And when you take prayer seriously, that's when God takes your prayers seriously.**

Different prayers are bold prayers (verses 29, 30). Having been bold in witness, they were equally bold in prayer. Notice what they didn't pray: they didn't pray for the Romans to go away; they didn't pray for the Sanhedrin to leave them alone.

Jesus never took the Romans away. Despite the Romans, Jews, and a lack of education and earthly resources, the followers of Jesus still turned the world upside down, and the church grew exponentially.

Get used to walking on water

Jesus did not calm all the storms either. He walked on the water in one of them. The second time He let the storm rage to teach the Twelve how to walk through chaos with confidence. *The chaos of the world around me does not negate the Word of God within me.* You and I should be walking on the water through the storm every single day. And I believe that's what God is doing in the church today.

Stop waiting for COVID to go away or for herd immunity to be achieved. As God said to Moses at the Red Sea, "Why are you crying out to me?" (Exodus 14:15). "Go forward!" Moses, looking at the sea, must have thought, *But God, this is different!* And God, reading his mind, must have winked and said, "Get used to different!" And they walked through the sea on dry land.

God may not remove COVID completely, even as He did not remove the Romans. Some died at the hands of the Romans and the Jews. Saul was the Jews' greatest weapon against the church—until Jesus got hold of him and turned him into Paul, the church's greatest hero, besides Jesus. (*And the devil's greatest nightmare.*) The devil didn't see that one coming! Oh, my friends, if we allow God to make us different, Satan will never see us coming either!

Now is the time to be different: To pray different. To think different. To not always wait for circumstances to be more favorable. To not wait for every obstacle to be removed; let the obstacles remain. Nothing stops God. "Enable your servants to speak your word with great boldness. Stretch out your hand to heal and perform miraculous signs and wonders through the name of your holy servant Jesus" (Acts 4:29, 30). That's the closing prayer we should be praying right now.

But today, instead of getting used to different, too many are fighting for all they're worth to return to the same. We can't possibly "do church" without gathering in our buildings, can we? We can't do evangelism without handbills and large venues for nightly in-person meetings, can we? We can't baptize souls coming to Jesus if they haven't been through all thirty lessons and are still struggling with addictions, can we? What if we run out of funds? What if we can't host our annual Christmas program? What if we have a resurgence of COVID and have to shut our doors again? Lord, carest thou not that we perish?

Hear God say to us today, "Why are you crying out to Me? Go forward!" Now, when the world needs the saving life and message of Jesus the most, is our time to shine. *These are not the times for business as usual because there's nothing usual about these times.* Jesus called us to be the salt of the earth, not the salt of the shaker. He said we are the light of the world, not the light of the church. Is it more difficult? Do we face greater challenges? Yes. But we should have been expecting this.

"The work which the church has failed to do in a time of peace and prosperity she will have to do in a terrible crisis under most discouraging, forbidding circumstances."[1] There's your storm that we, through the Holy Spirit, must walk through. Get used to different. But different doesn't mean defeat. It just means more determination in prayer for God to bring back His glory. It means praying for boldness and then being bold.

God is just as willing to stretch out His hand today to heal and perform miraculous signs and wonders of salvation through the name of His Son, Jesus, as He was then. But are we willing to stretch out our hands in prayer to receive those miracles? Are we willing to trouble ourselves to see normal become a thing of the past?

No, I don't believe God sent the coronavirus. But He allowed it. Just like He allowed the storm that night—the storm Jesus walked in. He could have said, "Peace, be still." But He didn't. Instead, He told Peter, "Come. Come out here with Me in this storm. You can walk on the water *if* you keep your eyes fixed on Me." And there, my friends, is the key to different—keeping our eyes fixed on Jesus.

Peter was successful at first. Peter actually walked on the water until, out of the corner of his eye, "he saw the wind" (Matthew 14:30) and became afraid. We know what wind represents in prophecy, right? Wind equals strife, war, and turmoil. When Peter saw the wind, he sank. Right now, during the storms of social, political, and conspiratorial unrest, there are a lot of "winds" blowing. And I'm afraid a lot of us are going down and sinking because we have taken our eyes off Jesus and are captivated and distressed by the wind. Stop it. Stop looking at the wind and the chaos and the confusion, and keep your eyes on Jesus. Only then will you be able to walk through the storm.

Getting used to different

God is presenting us with an opportunity to see things that have never been seen, hear things that have never been heard, and do things that have never been done.

"What no eye has seen,
    what no ear has heard,
and what no human mind has conceived"—
    the things God has prepared for those who love him—

these are the things God has revealed to us by his Spirit (1 Corinthians 2:9, 10).

What could be different about what God wants to reveal by His Spirit?

- How about church folk who actually love each other? *That would be different!*
- How about members who esteemed others as better than themselves and let no evil communication come from their mouths (or keyboards or smartphones or on Twitter or on Facebook)? *That would be different!*
- How about twenty- and thirty-year-old grudges being washed away with a towel and a basin of water, confessing faults to one another so that healing could take place? *That would be different!*
- How about baptizing people who accept Christ and are ready to follow Him without putting them on hold until we get them to sign off on thirty Bible lessons? *That would be different!*

   (And yes, I've heard the objections: they won't be "grounded," and we'll lose them. Are we keeping them now? If we offer them salvation and baptism first, what motive will there be to accept the Sabbath, the state of the dead, the sanctuary, veganism, and so on? Uh, how about love for Jesus?)

   What's the real reason we front-load the path to membership? Is it because we put our trust and resources in evangelists and pastors to teach and disciple while expecting nothing of our members?

- What if our pastors and evangelists brought people to Christ, and church members discipled them into the full message of "this new life" (Acts 5:20)? What if churches actually worked and made disciples as Jesus commanded? *That would be different!*
- How about a church alive, on a mission, where everyone had a sweet madness for Jesus, and you couldn't stop the members from telling others about Him if you tried? A church that made the devil tremble because of the prayers prayed, the souls saved, and the sins shunned? *That would be different!*

But all of this must be the new normal! Because that's what God is calling us to.

Let me tell you that the Lord will work in this last work *in a manner very much out of the common order of things,* and in a way that will be *contrary to any human planning.* There will be those among us who will always want to control the work of God, to dictate even what movements shall be made when the work goes forward under the direction of the angel who joins the third angel in the message to be given to the world. God will use ways and means by which it will be seen that He is taking the reins in His own hands. The workers will be *surprised by the simple means* that He will use to bring about and perfect His work of righteousness.[2]

Are you ready for different? To be surprised? For simple? Jesus says, "Follow Me." Before you can experience different, you have to *be* different, and Jesus wants to make you different. If you're willing, today's the day you get to walk on water.

Closing Prayer

Lord, I've got to be honest. I cling to "normal" and am terrified of different. But if it's You calling, let me come to You on the water. Show me things I've never seen before and surprise me with the simple means You will use to get us all used to different. Amen.

My Closing Prayer

Write yours here: ____

____

____

____

____

---

1. Ellen G. White, *Testimonies for the Church* (Mountain View, CA: Pacific Press®, 1948), 5:463.
2. Ellen G. White, *Testimonies to Ministers and Gospel Workers* (Mountain View, CA: Pacific Press®, 1944), 299; emphasis added.

8

PRAYING FOR RAIN

A long time passed. Then GOD's word came to Elijah. . . .
"I'm about to make it rain."

—1 Kings 18:1, The Message

Mercy drops. That's what they were—an earnest of showers to come. But for the people who had been praying earnestly for rain, the tears of desire and brokenness shed that morning were as significant as the "cloud as small as a man's hand" rising from the sea, spotted by Elijah's servant (1 Kings 18:44).

I was one of those praying on the daily prayer call that morning. It's still fresh in my memory, having happened only four days before this writing. Every morning at 8:00 A.M. (PST), a group of prayer partners from across the country come together on a phone line to worship and seek God for revival. As of this writing, the group has prayed daily, without a break, for more than 600 days straight.

Our coming together stemmed from a covenant of intercession on behalf of a colleague who was in deep distress. We made a pact that we wouldn't cease praying until God wrought deliverance for our friend. It wasn't long before it became apparent to everyone in the group that God had more for us to pray for. Was it a coincidence that we had been assembled at the beginning of the year that would reshape the world as we knew it through an invisible enemy called COVID-19? Hardly.

103

While the world stood still and the days morphed into weeks and months, the conviction grew that we had been called to pray for God's Spirit to move in revival. The deliverance finally came for our friend, but the intercession continued. More people and circumstances were added to our growing prayer list. We saw miracles and experienced disappointments. But always, there was encouragement, support, and the growing hunger to see God break through in our churches and communities in unprecedented power. We were living in the "splash zone" of the Spirit, as we liked to call it.

Then came the morning the Lord took over. Our usual pattern is to pray prayers of praise and thanksgiving at the beginning of the hour. Requests and testimonies are mingled in, and the fellowship is sweet. Someone is then chosen to give a fifteen- to twenty-minute devotional, which we affectionately call the "manna." We follow the manna with prayers of response, petitions, and prayers for the names on our intercession list.

But on this particular morning, God supplied the manna Himself. It started with a prayer of gratitude from one who was thankful for what God was doing in and through their ministry. Tears choked the one praying, and soon the mercy drops began flowing from my eyes and others' eyes. A fresh wave of intercession swept over our group, and spontaneous prayers of confession and praise and spiritual hunger rolled from person to person. The person scheduled to present the devotional that morning deferred and yielded the time to the Spirit, who was clearly in control. We knew we were in the presence of the King, and He was putting the prayers He wanted us to pray in our mouths.

Was it revival? No. But it was reviving. A taste. The first sprinkles of a promised rain we had been praying for. Mercy drops. That's what they were. But for a spiritual drought, such as the one we find ourselves in today, we must have more than dew. We need a downpour! Such was the case of Elijah the prophet.

Showdown on the mountain

It had been three and a half years since Elijah foretold the drought to Ahab in 1 Kings 17:1. Now in 1 Kings 18:1, the word of the Lord comes again to Elijah: "Go and present yourself to Ahab, and I will send rain on the land."

The Lord had declared an end to the drought, but before the rain would fall, God must first send fire to wake up His people. In the same way, *before we see the latter rain, God will need to set a holy fire under His people*—the fire of revival. Why? Because our Marah, our *anosognosia*, our spiritual narcolepsy, and our resistance to having our peace disturbed—all must be burned up!

When the king and Elijah finally come face to face, Ahab, who had initiated a massive yet unsuccessful manhunt for the prophet, said, "Is that you, you troubler of Israel?" (verse 17). Sometimes those suffering from extreme dehydration hallucinate and see things that aren't there. In this case, Ahab's spiritual dehydration was causing him to put the blame on the wrong person. He thought the drought was Elijah's fault when, in truth, it was his!

" 'I have not made trouble for Israel,' Elijah replied. 'But you . . . have. You have abandoned the Lord's commands and have followed the Baals' " (verse 18). A spiritual drought always follows when you abandon God's ways for man's. Our nation and church are suffering from a massive hallucination that is preventing us from seeing things as they really are. We are quick to blame the political party on the opposing side of our own, not realizing that we have put more trust in ________________ (fill in the blank) than in God. When this happens, the nation and the church become spiritual wastelands. And neither is as advertised.

You don't look like your picture

I was watching a sermon on YouTube earlier today that was preached by Terry K. Anderson in 2016. The sermon was titled "You Don't Look Like Your Picture." Pastor Terry starts the message by relating a story about being invited to preach in Newport News, Virginia. He had never been to Newport News and had not met the pastor of the church. The pastor knew Pastor Terry's appearance from a photo sent from Terry's church. The Virginia pastor was not available to make the airport pickup, so he sent a deacon in his place and gave him the picture of Pastor Terry so he would know who to look for.

While standing in baggage claim, Pastor Terry noticed a man looking at him. The two made eye contact, and then the man walked on past. About ten minutes later, the same gentleman came back to baggage claim and looked at the pastor, and the pastor looked at him. But once again, the man passed by without comment. This happened a third and fourth time. By now, Pastor Terry was getting nervous. "I don't like men looking at me too much," he says, drawing laughter from the congregation.

The last time the man came by, he finally approached and said, "Are you Pastor Anderson?"

"Yes sir, I am," replied Terry.

"I apologize," he said. "I passed by several times to pick you up. My pastor wasn't able to come, and he gave me a picture of you, but you don't look like your picture."

Pastor Anderson explained that he was about forty pounds lighter in that picture, had no gray hair, and his church had worn "all the pretty off."

"I would have gotten you sooner; I apologize, but you don't look like your picture."

Then Pastor Anderson homes in on his thesis for the message: "There is a portrait of the church in the New Testament book of Acts. And we have moved far from the DNA structure of the church in its infancy. The twenty-first-century church no longer looks like the first-century church. We have a whole lot of bells and whistles. We have buildings and budgets, parking lots and people, but for some reason, we don't look like our picture."[1]

This is what happens when spiritual dehydration afflicts a church. We're supposed to look like Christ, but we've put on too many pounds of pride; we've split so many theological hairs we have to wear wigs to cover our baldness. Furthermore, church and national politics, power struggles, prejudice, policies, and pettiness have worn all the "pretty" off. Like Israel in Elijah's time, we don't look like our picture. Dehydration is ugly. And Elijah called his people out for their dryness.

The dance

Ever try to straddle a road that eventually splits and widens as it forks in different directions? It's easy at first when the divergence is slight. You can walk on both roads with relative ease. As the gap between widens, you widen your stance to keep a foot on each road. Eventually, though, you have to hop or leap from road to road to cover the gap that has become wide enough to cause you to engage in quite the funny dance.

That is exactly what the Israelites were doing, except it wasn't funny. "How long will you *waver* ["limp" or "dance"] between two opinions? If the LORD is God, follow him; but if Baal is God, follow him" (1 Kings 18:21; emphasis added). The word *waver* is the same Hebrew word in verse 26, recorded there as "danced" when describing the priests of Baal as they hopped around the altar they had made. We all know what we mean when we refer to "church hopping": going from church to church without making a commitment to any. Israel was guilty of opinion hopping— dancing between Baal and Yahweh—without making a solid commitment.

Most people in the days of Elijah saw no problem with worshiping Yahweh and Baal. The worship of multiple gods—each having their respective spheres of responsibility—was common in the ancient world. Yahweh was the God of the Exodus and the God who led them in battles. The Baals and the Asherahs were the gods of fertility in humans, animals, and crops.

Plurality in worship had existed this way for centuries. But what was new was the militant promotion of Baal worship with Yahweh worship being made difficult. Jezebel was executing the Lord's prophets, and that's why Obadiah was hiding them in caves (verse 4)!

In today's post-Christian atmosphere, the Christian faith is increasingly confined to the church and family circle and is banned from the worlds of business and education and the marketplace of ideas. Christianity is being kicked to the curb and is only allowed to flourish behind closed doors. Ironically, the ideological doors of society are wide open to all manner of belief, nonbelief, and practice but not to God. God, it seems, belongs only to private life.

But if God really is God, He belongs to every sphere of life in every place and in every age. But this was not the reality of Elijah's times. His challenge to choose seemed strange, so "the people said nothing" (verse 21).

Their silence gave evidence that they weren't sure they wanted revival. They were happy with their version of the two-God two-step and weren't ready for the DJ (Elijah) to stop the music.

"Like a dark cloud, deception and blindness had overspread Israel. Not all at once had this fatal apostasy closed about them, but gradually, as from time to time they had failed to heed the words of warning and reproof that the Lord sent them. Each departure from right doing, each refusal to repent, had deepened their guilt and driven them farther from Heaven. And now, in this crisis, they persisted in refusing to take their stand for God."[2]

But *desperate times call for made-up minds.* In times of crisis, we don't need God hoppers; we need God seekers—those who will seek Him with *all* their hearts. James says that a double-minded man is unstable in all his ways (see James 1:8). "The one who doubts is like a wave of the sea, blown and tossed by the wind. That person should not expect to receive anything from the Lord" (verses 6, 7). If we pray for rain without made-up minds, uncommitted about who or what has our loyalty, we will receive nothing.

Do we want revival or not? Are we ready for rain, or are we content to be drought dwellers? The dance to have it both ways is killing the church. And it's exhausting.

The contest

Elijah proposed a contest and let the prophets of Baal go first. The odds appeared to heavily favor team Baal with a numerical advantage of 450 to 1. Each "team" got a bull and could prepare it for sacrifice on the altar of their choosing. The only thing they couldn't do is light the fire. They had to call on the name of their god, and the God who answered by fire—he was God (see 1 Kings 18:24). Because Baal was the god of storms and lightning, Elijah gave Baal the opportunity to act where he was supposedly strongest. Even the priests of Baal couldn't argue with the fairness of the contest, so they readily agreed.

Team Baal took the field first and even chose their own bull. "Then they called on the name of Baal from morning till noon. 'Baal, answer us!' they shouted. But there was no response; no one answered. And they danced around the altar they had made" (verse 26).

After several hours, Elijah began to get bored and started taunting team Baal. (In sports, this is called trash-talking.) Elijah urged them to shout louder. After all, Baal is a busy God. He had obviously been away on vacation the last three years during the drought, so he needed to be coaxed back from his holiday. He might have been napping or indisposed.

In response, team Baal amped up the decibels of their worship. "So they shouted louder and slashed themselves with swords and spears, as was their custom, until their blood flowed" (verse 28). This is what it can look like to have a form of godliness without any power. Many churches today have a lot of shouting and noise and frantic activity, but the Spirit of God is markedly absent. Team Baal was very religious and sincere (to the point of shedding blood!), but there was no response. No answer.

"Gladly would Satan have come to the help of those whom he had deceived, and who were devoted to his service. Gladly would he have sent the lightning to kindle their sacrifice. But Jehovah has set Satan's bounds, restrained his power, and not all the enemy's devices can convey one spark to Baal's altar."[3]

In false revivals and false worship, people may be moved, but God is not. God is moved by the simple, honest prayer of the humblest of His saints. He doesn't require a show, only humble faith and simple obedience. "*In repentance and rest* is your salvation, *in quietness and trust* is your strength" (Isaiah 30:15; emphasis added).

The restored altar

With the defeated prophets of Baal covered in their own blood and hoarse from shouting, Elijah takes the field. "Then Elijah said to all the people, 'Come here to me.' They came to him, and he repaired the altar of the Lord, which had been torn down" (1 Kings 18:30).

Desperate times call for a restored altar. "In ancient times men had at this altar worshiped the God of heaven, but for a long time it had not been used."[4] Its scattered stones were like the dry bones shown to Ezekiel—they were "very dry." The dry bones in the valley testified to the long absence of physical life. The scattered stones on Carmel testified to the long absence of spiritual life. The condition of the altar reflected the condition of the people.

The same is true today. We must tearfully confess that among the reasons for the darkness swallowing our children and our society is the broken family altar. Netflix, Xbox, unrestricted screen time, and so on have taken the place of prayer time at the family altar. Consequently, an entire generation has been sacrificed to the gods of entertainment.

"There are many homes today in which the altar of God has been broken down. It is time that a work be done similar to that upon Carmel. At evening God's children should reverently come together at the family altar for a period of quiet devotion. In the morning families should again unite in a season of prayer. The altar of prayer and devotion should be kept in constant repair."[5]

Each October in the conference where I serve, we engage in thirty-one days of family prayer. The vigil is called "Alter the Altar," and we supply families with daily resources to help them restore worship in the home. Praying for rain must begin at home.

As Elijah rebuilds the Lord's altar and prepares the sacrifice, each act reminds the people of God's covenant promise. The twelve stones and twelve jars of water remind them of the covenant promises given to their ancestors, the twelve patriarchs.

The prayer

"At the time of sacrifice, the prophet Elijah stepped forward and prayed: 'Lord, the God of Abraham, Isaac and Israel, let it be known today that you are God in Israel and that I am your servant and have done all these things at your command. Answer me, Lord, answer me, so these people will know that you, Lord, are God, and that you are turning their hearts back again' " (1 Kings 18:36, 37).

Desperate times call for the right prayer at the right time in the right way for the right reason.

Right prayer

Note who Elijah prays to—the Lord, the God of Abraham, Isaac, and Israel. Not to a false god but to the true God. The God of Israel. In the last days, another showdown looms between true and false worship. As we near the close of time, let's make sure the object of our worship is the Creator of heaven and Earth, not the lawmakers on Capitol Hill.

Right time

Note the time of the prayer—the time of the evening sacrifice. When God's time and our time align, miracles happen! It was the time of sacrifice—the time to worship God. It was also time for the drought to end. That's why Elijah is on Mount Carmel and not still by the brook Cherith. Brook time and Carmel time are two different times.

Make no mistake, the time Elijah spent by the brook was a miraculous time. Amazon and Uber Eats have nothing on God, who was the first to make air deliveries using a "fleet" of ravens to drop food to Elijah. This was a blessed time and a miracle time. But it was never intended to be permanent.

Our problem is our tendency to make idols out of everything, including the blessings of God. If left up to us, we would have erected a temple on that site and called it the "Church of the Immaculate Ravens." If something has worked in ministry—a particular outreach or a special season where God really showed up and blessed—we will make an institution out of it and never think of doing things another way. It's just the way we are.

God didn't allow Elijah to stay by the brook because He needed him at the altar on Carmel. Elijah wasn't to cling to a past experience, no matter how blessed that experience was. And this is why revival tarries: we're still praying brook prayers when it's time to pray for rain!

"We must pray that God will unseal the fountain of the water of life. And we must ourselves receive of the living water. Let us, with contrite hearts, pray most earnestly that now, *in the time of the latter rain*, the shower of grace may fall upon us. . . . If we pray for the blessing in faith, we shall receive it as God has promised."[6]

What time is it? It is time for the drought to end! We are "in the time of the latter rain." So stop living by the brook! It is time to "seek the Lord while He may be found" (Isaiah 55:6, NKJV). It is high time to awaken out of slumber. And don't overlook the word *sacrifice*. Restoring the altar of prayer and seeking God in the spirit and power of Elijah requires sacrifice. You won't just find time any more than Elijah just found Yahweh's altar. He was intentional and timely in his prayers, and we must be too.

Right way

Elijah's actions were according to the Lord's commandments. It wasn't an altar of his own making. He had done "all these things at *your* command" (1 Kings 18:36; emphasis added). Elijah could stand unashamed and unafraid before the multitude because he had heard the word of the Lord. That word had never failed. Had he not heard from God first, he would have every reason to be afraid. We should only be afraid if we haven't heard from the Lord and act according to our own ideas. Unlike the shrieks and gyrations of the prophets of Baal, Elijah spoke out of a relationship with a real and present God.

Right reason

Elijah prayed that the people would know that the Lord is God, repent, and turn their hearts back to Him. This is the *why* of our prayers. People need the Lord, and they need to repent.

Suzette and I were waiting for a table in a crowded restaurant one night (pre-COVID) when she asked me, "If you stood up right now and asked who is on the Lord's side, how many would stand?" I replied, "I think the general response would be, 'And who is the Lord?' " In these troublesome, godless times, we need to pray that God will show Himself to be the true and living God. We need to think more about the glory of God than our own personal comfort. Elijah didn't pray in order for his church to grow. He asked God to answer him so the people would know that the Lord was God!

Elijah's prayer was a model closing prayer because it marked the close of an era of apostasy and double-mindedness and opened an era of revival and reformation. The physical drought was ending along with the spiritual drought. If it is the "time of the latter rain," wouldn't that indicate that the time of our spiritual drought is at an end? What time is it, and what prayers are we praying?

> Then the fire of the Lord fell and burned up the sacrifice, the wood, the stones and the soil, and also licked up the water in the trench.
>
> When all the people saw this, they fell prostrate and cried, "The Lord—he is God! The Lord—he is God!" (verses 38, 39).

In Elijah, we see the omnipotent results of the human and the divine working in perfect harmony. "As the will of man co-operates with the will of God, it becomes omnipotent."[7] Such a contrast to the cold altars of idolatry and religious form. Is there fire on the altar of your church today? May our closing prayers at this last hour be omnipotent!

The sound of faith

But God wasn't through yet, and neither was Elijah. Carmel time was great and absolutely necessary. God answered by fire to rekindle the flame of devotion in His people, but He had promised rain. The miracle wasn't complete.

Elijah tells Ahab something strange and amazing. "Go, eat and drink, for there is the sound of a heavy rain" (verse 41). What sound is Elijah hearing? There was no sound of thunder overhead. There was no smell of rain in the air. There were no clouds. We know this because in verse 43, when Elijah told his servant to go look for signs of rain, there were none. There wasn't a cloud in the sky; nothing to indicate any imminent change in the weather. It was the same dry forecast they had seen for the last three and a half years.

So the question remains: when Elijah tells Ahab he hears the sound of a heavy rain, what sound is Elijah talking about? Hear me. Elijah doesn't need to hear thunder or the sound of approaching rain. Why? Because he has already heard the word of God. I submit that the only sound Elijah is hearing is the voice of God saying, "It's gonna rain!" And that's all Elijah needed to hear.

This is the sound of faith. As far as Elijah was concerned, it was raining already. And that's why Elijah could pray in confidence and didn't stop praying the first, second, third, fourth, fifth, or sixth time his servant came back with the report, "There's nothing there." God had spoken. It was done. It was just a matter of time.

Finally, after the seventh time, the servant reported, "A cloud as small as a man's hand is rising from the sea" (verse 44). "Let's go!" Elijah shouts. There is no hesitation. The prophet doesn't wait for the heavens to gather blackness; he doesn't wait for thunder. He acts on the first indication that his prayer had been heard.

What's the lesson for us who are praying closing prayers? *Desperate times call for persistent and prevailing prayer.* When the rain didn't immediately fall, Elijah's faith did not fail. His intercession did not cease. When there's no sign of change in the hearts of your loved ones or in your church or own life, keep praying. Why? Because there is the sound of a heavy rain! We have the word of God, and that's the only sound we need. It is the sound of faith. Hear Jesus say to you today, "Did I not tell you that if you believe, you will see the glory of God?" (John 11:40).

What's that sound I hear? It's Zechariah 10:1:

Ask the Lord for rain
In the time of the latter rain.
The Lord will make flashing clouds;
He will give them showers of rain,
Grass in the field for everyone (NKJV).

"God is as powerful, as willing, to grant victories today as He was in the days of Elijah. When God's people come to the place where they have the same spirit as Elijah had, when they are as earnest, as active, as courageous, as willing to persevere in prayer, as dauntless in the face of danger, and as eager to answer the calls of the Lord, then God's work will quickly be finished and Jesus will return to receive His own."[8]

In these days of Elijah, God is looking for ordinary men and women who will pray for rain. He's looking for people with made-up minds; people who will restore the family altar in their homes and lives; people who will pray the right prayer at the right time in the right way for the right reason; people who will pray and not give up; people who are getting used to different; people who aren't afraid of getting into good trouble; people who are praying, "Change me, search me, wake me, break me, and send me." Are you the one God is looking for? I pray I am.

The gift

I bought my grandson Jayden a football helmet and jersey for his sixth birthday. *(Go Hawks!)* Our daughter Candi FaceTimed us so we could see him open his present. I put on my helmet and jersey so he and his "papa" could be just alike.

Jesus gave us the gift of His Spirit so we could be like our Papa—our Abba. He gives us the helmet of salvation and the jersey of righteousness and the sword of the Spirit and all the rest so we can be just like Him!

About an hour after Jayden got his present, Candi sent us a text saying: "He is playing football all over the house and making Jesse talk like a sports commentator, reporting everything he does. LOL!" That's what Jesus wants to say to the Father about us: "Look! They are moving in the Spirit all over the place—in their homes, in their churches, in their workplaces, and in their communities. In everything they do, they are working and loving and praying and healing and living for Your glory, *just like Me*!"

Of course, I would have been happy if he wore his gift all day and even to bed! But sometimes, we take our uniforms off and on at will: on for church, off at home; on for Sabbath, off on the freeway, at work, or when we get around our friends.

God wants us to love the gift of His Spirit and keep His presence and power on at all times, especially in these times—the closing hours of Earth's history. This is the time of the latter rain. God wants to end the drought. Will you be God's Elijah and pray for rain?

At the beginning of this book, I told you about a retired pastor who asked me why we hadn't seen revival after all these years of praying. If we had that same conversation today, I would respond as Elijah did to his servant: "Go back and look again. The Lord has spoken. There is the sound of abundance of rain."

Closing Prayer

Lord, sometimes the only sound I hear is the sound of that wretched voice on repeat in my head, telling me I'm a hypocrite and I'll never be on par with Elijah. But that's not Your voice, is it? Help me to hear and obey only Your voice, Lord. You have promised rain, and I, for one, am thirsty! Make me willing to pray like Elijah and to prepare for the showers of blessing. "Mercy drops round us are falling, but for the showers," I plead![9]

My Closing Prayer

Write yours here: ____

____

____

____

---

1. Inspiration Station, "Rev. Terry K. Anderson – You Don't Look Like Your Picture (2016)," sermon by Terry K. Anderson, December 13, 2020, video, 44:01, accessed August 9, 2020, https://youtu.be/XTvp9KBfm1k.

2. Ellen G. White, *Prophets and Kings* (Mountain View, CA: Pacific Press®, 1943), 147.

3. White, 150.

4. Francis D. Nichol, ed., *The Seventh-day Adventist Bible Commentary* (Washington, DC: Review and Herald®, 1976), 2:819.

5. Nichol, 2:819, 820.

6. Ellen G. White, *Testimonies to Ministers and Gospel Workers* (Mountain View, CA: Pacific Press®, 1944), 509; emphasis added.

7. Ellen G. White, *Christ's Object Lessons* (Washington, DC: Review and Herald®, 1941), 333.

8. Nichol, *Seventh-day Adventist Bible Commentary*, 2:821.

9. Daniel W. Whittle, "Showers of Blessing," in *The Seventh-day Adventist Hymnal* (Hagerstown, MD: Review and Herald®, 1985), no. 195.

EPILOGUE: A CLOSING THOUGHT

A WHOLE LOT OF SHAKING GOING ON

I live in western Washington, about twelve miles from Seattle and a quick twenty-minute drive to Sea-Tac International Airport. When clouds permit, Mount Rainier, a magnificent but extremely dangerous volcanic mountain, dominates the landscape, reminding all who reside here that we live on the infamous Ring of Fire—a sprawling, horseshoe-shaped geological disaster zone in the Pacific. The ring stretches twenty-five thousand miles from New Zealand northward through Indonesia, the Philippines, and Japan to Alaska, then southward along the western coast of Canada and the United States down to South America. Western Washington is most definitely in an earthquake zone. As of May 4, 2021,

Washingtonians can get alert notifications on their phones when an earthquake is about to strike. . . .

Director of the Pacific Northwest Seismic Network Dr. Harold Tobin said the new ShakeAlert Earthquake Early Warning system will warn for earthquakes that could be dangerous.

"It has to reach a shaking intensity where pretty much everybody in a certain region is likely to at least feel it and potentially feel it as a moderate to even severe shaking," Tobin said.[1]

Having grown up in California, I've experienced several major quakes, and trust me, they're no fun. The few seconds bought by the ShakeAlert warning system could be just enough time for people to take cover and avoid serious injury.

Too bad there was no ShakeAlert technology in place for the "earthquake" of 2020 that shook the globe and claimed millions of lives. Even today, we are still feeling the aftershocks of the global pandemic, the most contentious presidential election in recent memory, racial reckoning, and an unthinkable assault on the United States Capitol. If only on January 1, 2020, we had all received a warning on our phones to take cover for the shaking to come, we might have been better prepared—but probably not.

Warnings of all kinds go largely unheeded until it's too late. Two millennia ago, Jesus warned of "great *earthquakes*, famines and pestilences in various places" (Luke 21:11; emphasis added) as signs of His coming. But students of prophecy have long known about another kind of shaking that has nothing to do with the seismic activity along the fault lines of planet Earth.

The shaking refers to a period of spiritual and doctrinal upheaval that rumbles through the church just before the time of trouble. This time of testing is likened to grain being shaken in a sieve to separate good kernels of wheat from the broken husks (chaff) surrounding them.

Under inspiration, the prophet Amos foretold a shaking among God's people: "For, lo, I will command, and I will sift the house of Israel among all nations, like as corn is sifted in a sieve, yet shall not the least grain fall upon the earth" (Amos 9:9, KJV).

When is this sifting to occur? How about now? "God is now sifting His people, testing their purposes and their motives. Many will be but as chaff—no wheat, no value in them."[2] "I saw that we are now in the shaking time."[3]

What are the causes?

- *Carelessness and indifference.* "The careless and indifferent, who did not join with those who prized victory and salvation enough to perseveringly plead and agonize for it, did not obtain it, and they were left behind in darkness, and their places were immediately filled by others taking hold of the truth and coming into the ranks."[4]
- *Persecution.* "As the defenders of truth refuse to honor the Sunday-sabbath, some of them will be thrust into prison, some will be exiled, some will be treated as slaves. . . .

"As the storm approaches, a large class who have professed faith in the third angel's message, but have not been sanctified through obedience to the truth, abandon their position and join the ranks of the opposition."[5]

- *Rejection of the Laodicean message.* "I asked the meaning of the shaking I had seen and was shown that it would be caused by the straight testimony called forth by the counsel of the True Witness to the Laodiceans. . . . Some will not bear this straight testimony. They will rise up against it, and this is what will cause a shaking among God's people."[6]
- *Superficiality.* "God's Spirit has illuminated every page of Holy Writ, but there are those upon whom it makes little impression, because it is imperfectly understood. When the shaking comes, by the introduction of false theories, these surface readers, anchored nowhere, are like shifting sand."[7]

Didn't see it coming

While I remain confident that the causes stated above are true, who knew that so many would be shaken by something other than Sunday laws? Something other than persecution? Just as the hack on the Colonial Pipeline exposed glaring security gaps and vulnerabilities in our nation's critical infrastructure, the politics and pandemics of the new decade have exposed alarming gaps in the faith of those awaiting the second coming of Christ. The earthquake of 2020 exposed our nakedness, though we thought we were clothed. It exposed our shallowness, though we prided ourselves on being deep. It exposed our readiness to cancel those who didn't share our views, even if they sat next to us in the same pew (six feet apart, of course!).

The tragedy is, despite the early warning system provided in Scripture, we still didn't see it coming. Not like this. It turns out that many were, like most American companies in this ransomware era, grossly underprepared to face these kinds of threats.

What's even more unsettling is the realization that these are but the foreshocks. God's answer to Jeremiah is fitting for us:

"If you get tired while racing against people,
     how can you race against horses?
If you stumble in a country that is safe,
     what will you do in the thick thornbushes along the Jordan River?"
          (Jeremiah 12:5, NCV).

Having been roughed up before the "*big* one" hits, while we are dusting ourselves off and assessing the spiritual damage we've incurred, what are the steps God is asking us to take to close the gaps between our profession and our practice? With the final crisis so close at hand, how then should we pray?

Jesus' prayer for Peter

On the last night of Jesus' life before His execution, He gathered His disciples for one final meal. The evening had gotten off to an awkward start with Jesus taking the role of a servant and washing the dirty feet of His disciples. As Jesus took the cup (the third cup of redemption) and proclaimed the new covenant in His blood, He warned of a betrayer. Talk about killing the mood! "They began to question among themselves which of them it might be who would do this" (Luke 22:23).

The sacred moment of the covenant was shattered by speculations of who was the rat among them. But to add insult to injury, "a dispute also arose among them as to which of them was considered to be greatest" (verse 24). *Really?* Jesus was hours from the cross, and they chose *that* moment to get into a fight about rank and honor. They didn't see the cross coming. They didn't see Gethsemane coming. They didn't see their own weak wills and sinful hearts. And they didn't see the enemy coming.

But Jesus did. After stopping the brawl with a lesson on what true greatness is, Jesus turns to His beloved Peter, who couldn't see his denials coming, and said, "Simon, Simon, Satan has asked to sift all of you as wheat." Peter was about to experience a shaking time. What could save him from being crushed in the time of trouble? "*But I have prayed for you, Simon, that your faith may not fail.* And when you have turned back, *strengthen your brothers*" (verses 31, 32; emphasis added).

The prayer that saved Peter in his shaking time is the same closing prayer that can save us from ours—that our faith will not fail and that we will strengthen (not strangle!) each other. And thank God, we're not left to pray this on our own. Jesus Himself is ever interceding for you and me that we grab hold of Him and never let go (Hebrews 7:25)!

I, for one, rejoice that when Jesus prays, I know the Father listens. Jesus said so Himself at the tomb of Lazarus: "Father, I thank you that you have heard me. I knew that you always hear me, but I said this for the benefit of the people standing here, that they may believe" (John 11:41, 42). Do you believe? Do I?

My prayer for you and for myself is that, during this time of shaking and quaking, our faith will not fail; it will be genuine and deep, not fake and shallow; we'll take the counsel of the True Witness and buy His gold refined in the fire to remove our poverty, His white clothing to cover our nakedness, and His eye salve to cure our spiritual blindness (see Revelation 3:18). "See to it, brothers and sisters, that none of you has a sinful, unbelieving heart that turns away from the living God. But *encourage one another daily*, as long as it is called 'Today,' so that none of you may be hardened by sin's deceitfulness" (Hebrews 3:12, 13; emphasis added).

A closing if

I want to close with the promise that started the journey of prayer for me in the mid-nineties:

"If My people who are called by My name will humble themselves, and pray and seek My face, and turn from their wicked ways, then I will hear from heaven, and will forgive their sin and heal their land" (2 Chronicles 7:14, NKJV).

God used those words to shake me then, and He's using them again to shake me now. What about you? So much has changed since the 1990s! Have we? Have I? For better or for worse? That question alone shakes me to my knees.

Time has not diminished the power or trustworthiness of 2 Chronicles 7:14. The offer still stands. The conditions remain the same. The result is just as certain. Only one thing stands between us and the change we seek—that tiny word *if*. How about it?

The world is all shook up. Don't let it shake your determination to claim all that God has for you *if* you really want it.

I've said enough.

The earth is moving.

Jesus is coming.

His will be done . . . *Amen.*

1. Abby Acone, "ShakeAlert Earthquake Warning System Goes Live for Washington State," KOMO News, May 4, 2021, https://komonews.com/news/local/shakealert-earthquake-warning-system-goes-live.

2. Ellen G. White, *Testimonies for the Church* (Mountain View, CA: Pacific Press®, 1948), 4:51.

3. Ellen G. White, *Testimonies for the Church* (Mountain View, CA: Pacific Press®, 1948), 1:429.

4. Ellen G. White, *Early Writings* (Washington, DC: Review and Herald®, 1945), 271.

5. Ellen G. White, *The Great Controversy* (Mountain View, CA: Pacific Press®, 1950), 608.

6. White, *Early Writings*, 270.

7. Ellen G. White, *Testimonies to Ministers and Gospel Workers* (Mountain View, CA: Pacific Press®, 1944), 112.

DISCUSSION GUIDE

Introduction: Opening Prayer

1. When you've prayed all kinds of prayers during the course of your life, what prayers do you pray when your time to pray is coming to an end?
2. Is the church in the western world reviving or regressing? Explain your answer.
3. What, according to the author, is the final crisis we need to be concerned about the most? Do you agree or disagree?
4. Jesus asked His disciples a loaded question: "When the Son of Man comes, will he find faith on the earth?" (Luke 18:8). Write about or discuss the things Jesus will surely find on the earth when He comes. What is the "faith" He's talking about, given the context of His entire teaching in Luke 18:1–8? Do you have this faith? Journal or discuss your answer.
5. How would you describe prayers of preparation for the final crisis?

Chapter 1: Change Me

1. If there was a word being blasted over and over again on social media and in the streets to describe the church during this unprecedented time of weirdness and upset, what would that word be? Write down the top three words that come to mind. Why those words?
2. How would you answer the question the retired pastor asked Randy: "After all the prayer conferences and prayer initiatives over the years, why haven't we seen revival yet?"
3. Read the poem by Wilbur Rees, titled "$3 Worth of God." What attitudes in this poem do you see reflected in the church today? Are there any attitudes in this poem that you see in yourself? Explain.
4. What does it mean to have revival without the Redeemer? What would that look like, and what would be the consequences?
5. Read 2 Corinthians 13:5. Why is this instruction necessary for those living in Earth's final hours?

6. Why did God lead the children of Israel to Marah? (See Exodus 15:25 and Deuteronomy 8:2.) Was this testing fair or unfair? Explain.

7. The root word of *Marah* means "deliberate, defiant, disobedience." Do you think you would have responded any differently than the Israelites did? How about now? Are you responding differently to today's Marah moment?

8. Some believers think that if they've been hurt or if someone disagrees with them, they get a pass to lash out with cutting words and scathing rebukes. Is that attitude defensible biblically? (See Ephesians 4:26, 31.) Are rage and revival compatible? Explain your answer.

9. Take a few moments to write down or discuss your response to this statement by Ellen White: "The 'time of trouble, such as never was,' is soon to open upon us; and we shall need an experience which we do not now possess and which many are too indolent to obtain" (*The Great Controversy*, 622).

10. Have you been born again? (Take your time to reflect prayerfully on this question before answering.) Does this question offend you? Examine your reaction, and journal your thoughts.

11. What is *anosognosia,* and how does this condition apply to you spiritually?

12. In light of this chapter, what closing prayer should we be praying?

Chapter 2: Search Me

1. The article cited at the beginning of this chapter references a retired Southern Baptist pastor who got caught up in QAnon conspiracies. This pastor is looking forward to the next Great Awakening. But he said that it wouldn't be like the other Great Awakenings, the religious revivals that torched through early America. This one would concern the state, not the church (Daniel Burke, "How QAnon Uses Religion to Lure Unsuspecting Christians"). Please discuss why this pastor's expectations are alarming or why they are not.

2. Is the author's warning to "be careful about the source of religious awakenings" valid? Why or why not? (Compare with Ellen G. White's statement from *The Great Controversy*, 462.)

3. List the end-time delusions talked about in Matthew 24 and 25:

   a. The delusion of _______________________ (Matthew 24:37–39, 42).

   b. The delusion of _______________________ (Matthew 24:45–50).

    c. The delusion of _______________________ (Matthew 25:1–13).

    d. The delusion of _______________________ (Matthew 25:14–30).

    e. The delusion of _______________________ (Matthew 25:31–46).

4. Which of the above delusions are more likely to trip you up than the rapture or being fooled by a fake christ? What makes you feel that way?

5. Read Psalm 139:23, 24. Have you prayed this prayer yourself? Would this be an appropriate prayer to pray at the end of time? Why?

6. Why do we need our hearts examined? (See Jeremiah 17:9.)

7. The author states, "If the human heart is the most deceitful of all things, then the greatest deception we need protection from is not coming from the left or the right or from the media but from *within*!" Do you agree or disagree? Discuss your answer.

8. Discuss Craig Groeschel's statement: "What I feared the most revealed where I trusted God the least." Is that true of you also? Write down the things you fear the most and then take them to God in prayer using 2 Timothy 1:7 as a guide.

9. Why is "see if there is any offensive way in me" a dangerous prayer to pray? How have you responded when God revealed something about you that needed cleansing? What is He revealing to you now?

10. Write down the four levels of inspection: heart, fears, sin, leading. Then ask God every day, What's in my heart, Lord? What am I afraid of? Where's the sin in my life that I'm holding onto? Where am I deluding myself? And then ask, What do You want me to do? Where do You want to take me with this? Write what you hear God saying to you.

Chapter 3: Wake Me

1. Describe primitive godliness.

2. How are the days of Noah like the days of COVID-19?

3. Prayerfully reflect on Luke 22:39–46. What temptation did Jesus want the disciples to watch out for?

4. When are we most vulnerable to temptation and sin?

5. Are you overwhelmed or exhausted emotionally and spiritually right now? Describe the source of your exhaustion and how it feels.

6. What are some of the consequences of sleeping instead of praying?

7. What does it mean to sleep through a revolution? Is the church in danger of this today? How so?

8. Do you agree with the pastor who shared this Facebook post: "Pray that

we won't go back to normal! Normal was killing the church in North America"? Discuss or journal your answer. What "normal" are you craving?

9. "There are some who, instead of wisely improving present opportunities, are idly waiting for some special season of spiritual refreshing by which their ability to enlighten others will be greatly increased. They neglect present duties and privileges, and allow their light to burn dim, while they look forward to a time when, without any effort on their part, they will be made the recipients of special blessing, by which they will be transformed and fitted for service" (Ellen G. White, *The Acts of the Apostles*, 54). How do you resemble this description? What do you and God need to talk about regarding this?

10. In what areas of your life are you spiritually asleep? Where is the spirit willing but the flesh weak?

Chapter 4: Break Me

1. Honestly, did you want to skip this chapter? If so, why?
2. What do you think the author means when he says, "There can be no Pentecost without Calvary"?
3. How has the pandemic broken us or exposed cracks in our Christianity?
4. Is it true that there can be no breakthrough without a breakdown? (See Joel 2:12–17.)
5. What is the role of anguish in spiritual breakthroughs?
6. Why are more people in anguish over the state of the economy or who's in the White House than they are over the state of the church or the state of their hearts?
7. If you will not be broken before God, it is inevitable that you will

____.

   Discuss or journal how this has been true in your life.
8. Why is it easier these days to boil over than to break down?
9. Discuss this statement by Oswald Chambers: "God can never make us wine if we object to the fingers He uses to crush us with. If God would only use His own fingers, and make me broken bread and poured-out wine in a special way! But when He uses someone whom we dislike, or some set of circumstances to which we said we would never submit, and makes those the crushers, we object. We must never choose the scene of our own martyrdom. If ever we are going to be made into wine, we will have to be crushed; you cannot drink grapes. Grapes become wine only when they have been squeezed" (*My Utmost for His Highest*, 202).

Do you like this statement? How are you being squeezed today?

10. To pray "Lord, break me" is to say, "Lord, ________________________."
11. Read Mark 14:3–9. What does the world smell from God's people who are being broken at this closing hour of Earth's history?

Chapter 5: Send Me

1. What does it mean to be "at peace in Laodicea"?
2. What three things did Isaiah see when he looked into the heavenly temple?
   a. God's ____________________________________
   b. His own __________________________________
   c. God's ____________________________________
3. Read Isaiah 6:2–4 and Revelation 4:2–11. The praise of God in heaven goes on 24/7 regardless of what happens on Earth. Why does this matter?
4. Read Isaiah 6:5. How can you tell whether people haven't seen themselves in the light of the holiness of God?
5. You cannot experience true conversion until you first realize your own ____. Do you agree or disagree? Can you support your answer with Scripture?
6. Read Isaiah 6:6, 7. Where is God's glory most clearly seen?
7. Why doesn't God use angels to proclaim His glory and represent Him?
8. Reflect on the prayer attributed to Sir Francis Drake, "Disturb Us, Lord." What makes this prayer hard to pray?
9. Where might God want to send you to represent Him?
10. To live and pray comfortably is to be a laughingstock to Satan's kingdom and a shame to God's. Please discuss or journal your response to this statement.

Chapter 6: "Good Trouble"

1. Why do you think God chose you to be alive now?
2. The late congressman and civil rights icon John Lewis famously said, "Never, ever be afraid to make some noise and get in good trouble, necessary trouble." What did he mean by that? What are the spiritual implications of this statement?
3. What is "the crystallization of discontent"?
4. Read the following stories: Mark 10:46–51; Mark 5:25–34; Mark 2:1–12. Journal or discuss how each of the principal characters

engaged in good trouble. In each case, was it also necessary? What made it so?

5. In each of the stories above, Jesus commended the individuals for their faith. What is the connection between faith and good trouble?

6. Read John 2:13–16, and reflect on Jesus' actions. Can they be justified? Why?

7. Sometimes effectual fervent prayer calls for us to disturb our peace, shake things up, flip some ideological tables, and "beat with violence at the very gates of heaven" (James Burns, *Revivals: Their Laws and Leaders*, quoted in Colin Whittaker, *Great Revivals*, 68). Do you agree or disagree with this statement? Share a time when you felt led to disturb the peace. How do you know whether it was justified?

8. "Only to those who wait humbly upon God, who watch for His guidance and grace, is the Spirit given. The power of God awaits their demand and reception" (Ellen G. White, *The Desire of Ages*, 672). What's the meaning of *demand* in this statement?

9. Are your prayers a disturbance to the kingdom of darkness? If not, why not? If so, explain why they are.

10. Define the words *languish* and *impenitent*. How do these words apply to the church? To you?

11. Discuss the reaction of the young people in an underground church in China to Francis Chan's description of the church in America. Why did they laugh? Was that reaction justified? Does Satan laugh too? How does that make you feel? How do you think Jesus feels about it?

12. What are the keys to Heaven-interrupted praying?

    a. ____

    b. ____

    c. ____

    d. ____

    e. ____

    f. ____

    g. ____

    h. ____

    i. ____

    j. ____

    k. ____

13. Journal or pray your way through each of the keys listed above.

14. What is God asking you to do in light of this chapter?

Chapter 7: "Get Used to Different"

 1. Why is it such a tragedy for Christians to have such low expectations, to always play it safe, and to keep repeating things the way we've always done them?

 2. How are lameness and lukewarmness similar?

 3. How can we stop being "lame"?

 4. Why does "different" faith upset those who don't have any?

 5. When do you take Jesus seriously, and why? Why is being average, normal, and spiritually flabby pretty OK by most Christian standards?

 6. Read Acts 4:24–31. Why didn't the believers pray for the Romans to go away or for the Sanhedrin to leave them alone?

 7. What closing prayer should we be praying right now?

 8. Why didn't Jesus calm the storm before Peter walked on the water? (See Matthew 14:22–31.)

 9. What are some "winds" causing Christians to sink in the storm? What's the key to walking through the storm?

10. Ellen White said, "Let me tell you that the Lord will work in this last work *in a manner very much out of the common order of things,* and in a way that will be *contrary to any human planning.* There will be those among us who will always want to control the work of God, to dictate even what movements shall be made when the work goes forward under the direction of the angel who joins the third angel in the message to be given to the world. God will use ways and means by which it will be seen that He is taking the reins in His own hands. The workers will be *surprised by the simple means* that He will use to bring about and perfect His work of righteousness" (*Testimonies to Ministers and Gospel Workers,* 299; emphasis added).

    How do you react to this statement? What are the implications for your church? How can you pray differently in light of these words?

Chapter 8: Praying for Rain

 1. How would you describe your own spiritual state right now? Circle the answer that best fits your experience:

"Mercy Drops"   "Drought"   "Abundance of Rain"

Explain your answer to the group or in your journal.

2. Why did God have to send fire before the promised rain to end the drought? What kind of fire is needed in your life today?

3. Consider Pastor Anderson's statement: "There is a portrait of the church in the New Testament book of Acts. And we have moved far from the DNA structure of the church in its infancy. The twenty-first-century church no longer looks like the first-century church. We have a whole lot of bells and whistles. We have buildings and budgets, parking lots and people, but for some reason, we don't look like our picture" (Terry K. Anderson, "You Don't Look Like Your Picture").

   Do you agree or disagree with him? Explain.

4. As a believer, in what ways do you not look like your picture?

5. Describe the two-God two-step. Have you ever "danced" between two opinions like the children of Israel? In what ways are you doing the dance even now? Pause and pray about this.

6. Why is it necessary to have a made-up mind in preparation for the final crisis?

7. Why was it important for Elijah to restore the Lord's altar? What is the condition of your own family altar? If it is in disrepair, what can you do to restore it?

8. What is the right prayer at the right time in the right way for the right reason? How can we begin praying this way in our churches?

9. Talk about the concepts of brook time and Carmel time. What makes those two times different, and what are the consequences of praying "brook" prayers when it's time to pray for rain?

10. Why was Elijah's prayer (1 Kings 18:36, 37) a model closing prayer?

11. "As the will of man co-operates with the will of God, it becomes omnipotent" (Ellen G. White, *Christ's Object Lessons*, 333). What does this mean in practical terms? If this is true, what are the ramifications and what is God asking us to do about them?

12. What is your own experience with the sound of faith? What have you believed in your heart despite not seeing evidence with your eyes? What sound should we be paying attention to today?

13. At the end of the chapter are listed some of the prayers God wants ordinary men and women to pray. Of those listed, which ones are the most difficult for you to pray? Why? Which are you most ready to pray? Why?

14. As you conclude this book, what *one* thing do you feel compelled to do based on everything you've read?